DR. WARREN WIERSBE
        PASTOR, AUTHOR, CONFE̶R̶E̶N̶C̶E̶ ̶S̶P̶E̶A̶K̶E̶R̶

"As society's false views of success invade our homes and churches, they erode Christian character. *The Success Fantasy* explains how this is happening, and why, and what we must do about it. I hope every Christian—especially parents, pastors, and teachers—will listen to what Tony Campolo says. We need to stop living on substitutes and get back to reality."

DR. WILLIAM J. KEPHART
PROFESSOR OF SOCIOLOGY,
        UNIVERSITY OF PENNSYLVANIA

"*The Success Fantasy* is no fantasy! It's for real. Dr. Campolo has reached far and wide—his repertoire is immense—and what he has to say should be of value to all Americans. This book will make you richer, not materially, but in the sense of leading a more meaningful and gratifying life."

L. D. JOHNSON, CHAPLAIN,
        FURMAN UNIVERSITY

With pithy wit and natural humor, Tony Campolo has written a penetrating analysis of the contemporary idolatry of Success. But this is more than analysis. It is a passionate plea for the claims of Christ upon our value system.

Campolo's understanding of the plight of the 'little people,' of the adolescent who is struggling to grow up, and especially of the young woman who is treated as a sex object, is insightful and illuminating. Tony Campolo writes like he speaks. He hits hard but with humor and always with a redemptive note of love.

Anthony Campolo, Jr.

The Success Fantasy

This book is designed for your personal reading pleasure and profit. It is also designed for group study. A leader's guide with helps and hints for teachers and visual aids (Victor Multiuse Transparency Masters) is available from your local bookstore or from the publisher.

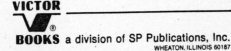

VICTOR

BOOKS a division of SP Publications, Inc.
WHEATON. ILLINOIS 60187

Offices also in
Whitby, Ontario, Canada
Amersham-on-the-Hill, Bucks, England

Sixth printing, 1984

Cover photo by Camerique

Scripture quotations are taken from the *New American Standard Version* © 1960, 1962, 1963, 1968, 1971, 1972, 1973, the Lockman Foundation, La Habra, California. Used by permission. Other versions used are the King James Version; the *New International Version* © 1978 by the New York International Bible Society; *The Holy Bible in the Language of Today* by Dr. William F. Beck, copyright © Mrs. William F. Beck, 1976, published by A. J. Holman Company. Used by permission. *The New Testament in Modern English* © J. B. Phillips 1958, The Macmillan Company.

Recommended Dewey Decimal Classification: 248.4, 301, 261.83
  Suggested Subject Headings: CHRISTIAN ETHICS; BEHAVIOR

Library of Congress Catalog Card Number: 79–67852
ISBN: 0–88207–796–1

VICTOR BOOKS
A division of SP Publications, Inc.
  Wheaton, Illinois 60187

CONTENTS

To my mother, Mary Campolo, who always said, "Go over the top for Jesus!"

FOREWORD

One of the serious problems of our day is that so many people compare their successes to false standards. Even when they achieve their goals, they feel empty and emotionally bankrupt, because they have not put their work alongside of God's measurements for success.

Tony Campolo is a prophet with practical ideas you can put to work in your everyday life. This book captures what Tony does best— weaving together sound biblical theology, practical sociology, and workable psychological insights.

Tony Campolo is a favorite resource person for conferences of the Youth for Christ professional staff. I think you will enjoy reading *The Success Fantasy*.

Jay Kesler, President
Youth for Christ International

1
What
Is Success?

Success is a shining city, a pot of gold at the end of the rainbow. We dream of it as children, we strive for it through our adult lives, and we suffer melancholy in old age if we have not reached it.

Success is the place of happiness. And the anxieties we suffer at the thought of not arriving there give us ulcers, heart attacks, and nervous disorders. If our reach exceeds our grasp, and we fail to achieve what we want, life seems meaningless and we feel emotionally dead.

Since failure is our unforgiveable sin, we are willing to ignore all forms of deviance in people if they just achieve the success symbols which we worship. Therefore, while we send those guilty of petty crimes to penitentiaries, we honor our robber barons by calling them *philanthropists* and naming universities and churches after them.

What is success? The word means many things, but for the sake of our discussion, let us agree that in our culture *success* means an individual has gained for himself one, if not all, of the following: wealth, power, and prestige. Sociologists teach us that wealth, power, and prestige express a "strain to consistency." This means that when people possess one of these, they tend to have the other two also. The wealthy tend to have power and prestige. The powerful usually gain prestige and wealth, and the prestigious are likely to be people of wealth and power. People who have only one of these attributes will seldom be content until they have the other two. In our society, the usual path to success is first to acquire wealth and then gradually to gain prestige and power.

Wealth

Who would question that wealth is a major proof of success? Those who have it are treated with deference and honor, while those who lack it are usually relegated to social insignificance and, at times, to disgrace.

Christians in the early church, who should have known better, often gave preference to the rich and humiliated the poor. James, in his epistle, cited such practices and condemned them:

> For if a man comes into your assembly with a gold ring and dressed in fine clothes, and there also comes in a poor man in dirty clothes, and you pay special attention to the one who is wearing the fine clothes, and say, "You sit here in a good place," and you say to the poor man, "You stand over there, or sit down by my footstool," have you not made distinctions among yourselves, and become judges with evil motives? Listen, my beloved brethren: did not God choose the poor of this world to be rich in faith and heirs of the kingdom which He promised to those who love Him? But you have dishonored the poor man. Is it not the rich who oppress you and personally drag you into court? (James 2:2–6)

When people fail, they may feel that even God rejects them. Many have found it difficult to believe they are acceptable to the Almighty, after they have been proven unacceptable by the success criteria of our culture.

Many people have twisted the Judeo-Christian message to mean that wealth is evidence of superior spiritual stature. Some

Christians make the amount of money a person possesses a means of judging his relationship with God, pointing out that when the ancient Jews were right with God, they enjoyed such an abundance of things that their cups were full and overflowing. They say that if we keep the Law of God, particularly His command to tithe one tenth of our income to the work of the church, the Lord will prosper us beyond our imagination. Such claims are made in spite of the fact that there are tens of thousands of people in Third World nations who love the Lord, obey His Law, faithfully tithe, and yet suffer privation beyond our comprehension. Many Christians subconsciously believe that God must be in league with the rich person.

As a boy I remember attending testimony meetings at our church where Christians told how they were poor and beaten people until they accepted Christ as personal Saviour and Lord. Then they would relate how, as a consequence of their new lives in Christ, they suddenly experienced prosperity. Those testimonies always intrigued me because Jesus taught that following Him would cost us everything we possessed and that in the end, we could find ourselves—like the Apostle Paul—poor, battered, and imprisoned.

Sermons from the pulpit, articles in magazines, and testimonies of successful Christian businessmen at luncheon meetings, all reinforce the creed that Jesus will prosper us if we just walk in His ways. An exaggerated example of this belief is the television preacher, Reverend Ike. On more than one occasion, he has said: "God doesn't want anybody to be poor. If you believe in Him you will believe in yourself, and if you believe in yourself, you will get rich. I'm rich and that's because I believe in God and I believe in Reverend Ike."

In our society many people ultimately measure a person's worth by the amount of wealth possessed at death. We have all heard people say about someone who has just died: "He was born poor with humble parents, but by the time he died he was worth millions of dollars.'' It is as if that is the best thing that can be said about the person.

We even look for the symbols of wealth at the time of death. This is why we provide such lavish funerals. Even if the person was not rich, we want him to appear so in his final display before friends and relatives.

I heard of a funeral in California where a man requested to be buried seated behind the wheel of a brand new Cadillac, dressed in a tuxedo, with a two-dollar cigar in his mouth. He left the money to insure that his wish would be fulfilled, and when he died his plan was carried out. The undertaker brought in a huge crane to maneuver the automobile which served as the casket for the dead man. As he pulled the handle lowering the corpse and Cadillac into the ground, the crane operator was heard to say, "Man, that's really living!"

One time my daughter and I were taking the Grayline Bus Tour of Chicago. As our bus stopped in front of a movie theater, our guide pointed to an alley, and in a sober manner told us it was there that John Dillinger, the infamous bank robber, was gunned to death by the FBI. Then he added, "When John Dillinger died, after robbing more than one million dollars from banks across the Midwest, he had only thirty-two cents left to his name."

My daughter responded, "What great timing!"

In her opinion, if you have to die, what better time to go than just when the cash is running out? But Americans do not generally share that opinion. For many, nothing could be worse than to have the final syllables describing existence be the condemning phrase, "He died penniless."

Power

Because we want to determine our own destinies, we resent upheaval from forces beyond our control. We enjoy having people be subservient to us, and deem ourselves powerful if we can direct the actions of others.

As Christians we may say we want power in order to do good for others in Christ's name. We may claim that our sole motivation for seeking power is that we see what needs to be done and want a free hand to do it. On such a noble platform, we seek high offices and important appointments. But such purity of purpose is usually more declaration than reality. All who seek power have covert desires which have to do with the ego gratification that possession of power brings.

I have never held power in any significant way, but I did win a primary election, which made me a candidate for the U.S. Congress. While I lost the general election, the very fact that I had been a candidate for my congressional district gave me a certain amount of influence over some minor politicians who held patronage jobs in our district.

At times people in deep trouble would come to me, after they had been unable to get the local political bureaucracy to respond to their needs. I used to love reaching for the phone, calling the bureaucrat who had been causing the problem, and ordering him to do things right—or else. When the troubled person would look at me with gratitude and admiration, I would try to convince myself that my motives were pure; but down deep inside, I had an inkling that I enjoyed the use of my power too much to consider the act purely altruistic.

In many respects, the feminist challenge to the traditional roles of men and women has turned into a power struggle. Husbands who feel victimized in their everyday jobs are reluctant to lose their authority in the home. They hang onto power tenaciously, using the Bible to legitimate the domination of their wives and children.

On the other hand, there are women who feel no sense of significance because they feel that they are under the control of their husbands. Such women resent having to wash the dishes, scrub the toilets, and change the diapers while their husbands sit enthroned in comfort, reading the newspaper. These women claim that because they are being treated as servants, they must rebel.

In labor disputes, the issues often have less to do with money than with labor's resentment of "management's indiscriminate use of power." The workers want to determine what can and cannot be done to them by the management. They want to be part of the decision-making process. Employers know that frequently an unhappy employee can be appeased without a raise in salary, as long as he is given an increase in power.

Many a foreman has quit his job in frustration because the unions have curtailed his ability to tell the workers what to do. Without power, there does not seem to be much reason to continue on the job, in spite of an attractive salary.

Even the church cannot escape from petty struggles for power. No one can tell how many churches have disintegrated into power struggles, splitting congregations or causing systemic groups to pull out of the church. The spokesmen for the warring camps usually cloak their actions in such idealistic claims as "standing for truth" or "being faithful to the Gospel." But we are all too aware that behind such conflicts are people vying for power.

Even as we seek power, we sense something inherently wrong with what we are doing. We are confronted by our Lord Jesus Christ who stands in opposition to our power plays.

During Jesus' temptation (Matt. 4), Satan tried to lure Him into utilizing power in ways that would compel people to grant Him allegiance by:

• feeding them bread made from stones,

• astounding them as He floated down from the temple pinnacle and landed unhurt,

• establishing earthly authority over the systems and peoples of the world.

But Jesus refused to use power to win followers. Instead, He emptied Himself of power and chose to win us from a position of weakness—the Cross. The Scripture says that He became an obedient Servant, obedient unto death, "even death on a Cross" (Phil. 2:8). He was born in weakness and He died in weakness; for through that weakness, the Father worked His will in history, as salvation became a reality. Christ wants us to give up our power plays and attempts to dominate others, and to follow Him into servanthood.

A world that worships power, and sees it as an ultimate mark of success, has a hard time comprehending a kind of success that is based on the mutual submission of love. Frederick Nietzsche, the atheistic, existentialist philosopher, claimed that the "will to power" was the most basic drive of the human personality, motivating all of human behavior. I believe there is more to Nietzsche's claim than we want to admit. Power *is* a mark of success within our society, and the human appetite for it seems insatiable.

Prestige

If we lack money and power, we can still feel successful if we have the respect of our peers. As a young minister without wealth or power, I loved to be called "Reverend." It was an ego trip for me when I was asked to pray at important public gatherings; I thrilled at the honor of addressing prestigious meetings. When I was asked to fly from Pennsylvania to speak at a convention on the West Coast, that seemed proof that I was somebody special. I might be short on power and low on cash, but I felt as successful as any millionaire or congressman when I just "humbly" preached the Gospel to a few thousand people.

Employers joke about the fact that if they can't give employees a raise in salary, they can satisfy them with more prestigious titles. At social gatherings, we love to impress people by convincing them that we hold important positions. We feel successful if people are impressed upon hearing our answer to the question, "What do you do?"

We all play for prestige. Clergymen seek honorary degrees to write after their names. High school boys pay a high price to be known as part of the varsity football team. Young girls fantasize over the status they will enjoy when the gang at school knows whom they are dating. We all tend to play one-upmanship with each other, and at the same time claim to be followers of Jesus who "made Himself of no reputation" (Phil. 2:7, KJV).

Feeling successful by means of prestige is a complex problem for women. Traditionally, they obtained their prestige vicariously, by borrowing it from their husbands. If their husbands had jobs that brought positive recognition, the women felt that they too were important. However, the feminist movement is changing all of that, saying each woman should have her own accomplishments to earn the respect of others.

For many a woman, this call to individual success has come too late. She has been comfortable in sharing her husband's successes, content to smile benevolently as he receives honors at the Kiwanis Club meeting and graciously tells the crowd, "I would not be here today if it weren't for my dear wife who has stood by me through thick and thin, and supported me in all my endeavors."

It seems like a dirty trick to play on such women. After becoming used to feeling successful because they are married to successful husbands, they are now told that it won't do any more. They are informed that this age requires each woman to earn status through her own achievements. Such a challenge can create insecurities, particularly for women over 40 years of age.

When I evaluate my own attitudes, I find that the only time I am seriously tempted to lie is when it will enhance my personal status. I have a tendency to make myself out as more than I really am, to paint myself bigger than life. I exaggerate my successes, minimize my failures, and offer myself to the world as somebody who has done great things. Oh, what a sorry contrast I make to Jesus who was willing to make Himself nothing for our sakes! God honors the humility of His Son by giving Him "the name which is above every name, that at the name of Jesus every knee should bow . . . and every tongue confess that Jesus Christ is Lord (Phil. 2:9–10).

Those who seek prestige will never get it from God; but those who are willing to be humble and take "the inferior seats at the banquet" will find that the heavenly Father calls them to the places of honor which they know they do not deserve. (See Luke 14:7–11.) The Scripture warns that those who seek the praise of the world have their reward here on earth, but those who are willing to serve in secret, without any thought of public recognition, will find themselves honored in heaven (Matt. 6:1–6).

Christians and the Big Three

Because the world sees wealth, power, and prestige as the indicators of success, we have been conditioned to seek them with all of our might. But our Lord has different criteria for evaluating success. He calls us away from society's symbols of success and urges us to seek after "His kingdom and His righteousness" (Matt. 6:33). Many who are considered least important by society may find themselves sitting in places of honor at the great banquet feast in the world to come.

Wealth, power, and prestige can corrupt those who possess them. *Wealth* can delude us into a kind of self-sufficiency and denial of our need of God. It is easy to become so overly protective of our economic interests that we oppose compassionate social policies which would diminish our wealth.

Power can turn us into megalomaniacs. Desire to dominate others can lead us to diminish their humanity, as well as our own. Sometimes we sacrifice those who are nearest to us, in order to achieve power.

Cravings for *prestige* can lead us into destructive pride and egotism that know no bounds, until our need for the world to focus on us becomes obnoxious.

Yet we must remember that wealth, power, and prestige have great potential for good. It is only their wrong use which is evil. Our Lord owns the cattle on a thousand hills and the wealth in every mine. He has the power to hold the universe together or to destroy it in an instant. But He uses His wealth, power, and prestige to express love and to benefit everyone.

If we wish to be governed by God's will, we can learn to use our wealth, power, and prestige for others, and to extend the kingdom of God in the world.

2
Successful People Can Be Disciples

It is not necessary to be a failure in order to be a follower of Jesus. Successful people are also called to follow after the Master. The Scripture teaches that those holding trophies of success must be willing to lay them at the foot of the Cross, willingly surrendering their wealth, power, and prestige to Jesus. It is a beautiful thing to see people who are willing to use the success they have earned in obedience to the will of God.

Do You Feel like a Failure?

There are not many people who truly feel successful. One of the great ironies in this world is that those who achieve great success in the eyes of others often feel like failures themselves. We all know people who seem driven to achieve more and more to convince themselves that they are successful. In a sense that was the basic problem of President Nixon. Regardless of what others may say, I believe he is basically a good man. His downfall resulted from the fact that he never felt himself to be completely successful, no matter what he achieved.

It was this that led to Watergate. For Nixon it was not enough to be a successful candidate; he craved a total victory that would be a complete mandate to power. He wanted election results that would declare him so popular that his cravings for self-affirmation would be satisfied. But in the end, this desire for affirmation drove him to self-destruction.

The Significant Other

What is it that gives us a sense of satisfaction about our successes? What is it that makes some people feel successful—in spite of the fact that the world in general declares them to be failures, while others have a sense of failure—in spite of the fact that the world thinks them successful? The answers to these questions lie in one important truth: *We are successful if the most significant people in our lives deem us successful.*

Perhaps we all know a man who has accomplished great things but lacks any sense of self-fulfillment because he has not achieved success in the eyes of his father. If that father is the *significant other* in his life, the applause of thousands will not mean as much to him as the recognition that could be given by that one person, his own father.

I know a woman who is a fantastic pianist and widely known as an accomplished artist. Nevertheless, she feels a deep sense of failure because her father, also a famous pianist, has never given her the approval she desperately craves. She works incessantly and suffers constantly, striving to gain success in his eyes. Wealth, power, and prestige mean nothing without the approval of the ones we love.

The lover knows that success means being viewed as successful in the eyes of his or her significant other. I remember the lyrics of a song from my teenage years that went something like this:

If they made me a king, I'd still be a slave to you.
If I had everything, I'd still be a knave to you.
If I ruled the earth, what would life be worth,
If I hadn't the right to you?

Progressive Significant Others

At different stages of our lives, the significant others change. Those persons whose approval gives us the inner feeling of success are not the same throughout the life cycle. Children will puff up with pleasure when they do something that makes "Mommy and Daddy" proud of them. Nothing destroys them more or leaves them with a greater sense of failure than an awareness that their parents disapprove of what they have done. As a boy, I remember rushing home with a good report card to be praised by my mother and father. If they said that I was a good boy because I had done well, I knew that there was nothing more to be achieved. My life revolved around this parental approval.

For teenagers, the significant others tend to be in their peer groups. Most of us can recall periods in our lives when the approval of "the gang" supplanted the opinions of parents. We may even have developed an indifference to parental approval and looked with disdain on those high school classmates who were still primarily motivated by a desire to please their parents.

Our male chauvinistic society has been particularly hard on boys who work overtime to gain the praise of their mothers. They have been called "Mama's boys" and regarded as far less "macho" than most boys imagine themselves to be.

The years of passage into adulthood are years when the significant others are young people of their own age group. If *they* think a person is "cool," then he is bathed in the ecstasy of feeling successful. And then too, the disapproval of parents can easily be endured.

As I think back to my own teen years, I know that of all the members of the peer group who gave me a sense of significance, none were more important than those of the opposite sex. Girls who were popular with the boys felt like successful "somebodies." Nothing diminished a girl's sense of worth more than to lack a high rating with the boys at school.

Among the boys there was a willingness to do anything to earn the admiration of special girls. I remember going out for every team hoping that my athletic prowess would make the girls I liked worship me. I fantasized constantly about scoring the winning touchdown, dropping the winning basket through the hoop just as the gun went off in the tournament game, or winning the cross-country championship with a sudden burst of speed, overtaking my opponents just before the finish line. For me the games were only a means to the end—and that end was to win more approval and admiration from the girls than any of the other guys. Success meant gaining the approval of my peers, particularly my female peers. They had replaced my parents as the significant others in my life.

The Generalized Other

When trying to define the significant others for adults, we have a more complicated task. We are not quite sure whose approval adults try to gain. It is too simple to say that, like teenagers, they want to impress their peers. Adults want more than that. They want approval from the world in general. They want people whom they have never met to know of them and admire them. Adults wish to enjoy wide recognition and universally recognized symbols of success.

George Herbert Mead, a prominent, early 20th-century sociologist, used the expression *the generalized other* to denote that amorphous group toward which adults orient their behavior. How often do we act in a particular manner in order that "they" might approve of us? When we think of failure, we fear that "they" will despise us. It is before this nonspecific jury that we plead our case for personal worth. It is the verdict we think "they" pass on us that holds the basis for our well-being.

But who are *they*—these persons who hold our sense of self-worth so carelessly in their hands? *They* are everybody, and yet *they* are nobody special. *They* are people we have never met, but who may prove to be the most important persons in our lives. Those whom Mead called the *generalized otner*, Nietzsche called the *herd* and the Bible calls the *world*. For adults, the generalized other becomes the significant other whose praise gives feelings of success.

Competition and Fear of Failure

We respect success more when it is competitively achieved. Those who inherit wealth, power, and prestige are not looked upon as true fulfillers of the American Dream. Somehow they seem to lack the virtues of truly successful people who have earned these things on their own.

In this competitive struggle, which all of us seem compelled to enter, there is the constant fear of failure. And it is this fear of failing which elicits some of our most pathetic behavior. The child, afraid that he has not done enough to earn the approval of his parents, will boast of achievements that were never his, or exaggerate what he has accomplished. The teenager, aware that acceptance by his peers must be carefully engineered by imitating their lifestyles, lives in fear that he might do, say, or even think something that would leave him alienated and alone. The adult who isn't quite sure whom he is trying to please, has fears that turn into diffused anxiety, leaving him immobilized and incapable of taking the risks necessary for a fulfilled and successful life.

Another Option

Christianity provides an alternative to the threats of failure that loom so large in our success-hungry society. There is deliverance from the fears that sap the joy from living. The Gospel is the Good News that there is another option which keeps the success game from being the only game in town.

When we become Christians, we invite Jesus to be the Significant Other in our lives. We allow Him to displace the generalized other, in the language of Mead; or the world, in the language of the Scriptures. To be *Christian* means that we seek His approval and learn to count what the world says about us as secondary. It is difficult to please both Jesus and the generalized other at the same time. As Christians, our ultimate calling is to do "that which is pleasing in His sight" (Heb. 13:21).

When we orient ourselves to Jesus, seeking to gain His approval, we will discover that we are accepted just as we are. Jesus does not require some great achievement before He affirms our worth. To each of us He says, "If you had been the only person who ever lived in time and history, you are so precious to Me that I would have died to save only you."

We don't have to work to gain positions of privilege at His right hand, for He has already declared us to be heirs of God and joint heirs with Him. This means that ultimately, the wealth of the universe is ours. It means we have been assigned a status higher than the angels. It means we receive power to join the family of God, and to serve man and God according to His will.

It is difficult for North Americans to believe these truths because of the idea that success is competitively earned. We find it hard to be the heirs of spiritual wealth, power, and prestige. We want to do something wonderful for God, to be deserving of these things.

St. Paul tried to convince the early Christians that "by grace you have been saved through faith; and that not of yourselves, it is the gift of God; not as a result of works, that no one should boast" (Eph. 2:8–9). We go through life tortured by the belief that we have not done enough to be worthy of His approval, in spite of the fact that He tells us we are approved by Him because of what His Son has done on our behalf. Nothing can take His loving approval away from us. "Neither death, nor life, nor angels, nor principalities, nor things present, nor things to come, nor powers, nor height, nor depth, nor any other created thing, shall be able to separate us from the love of God, which is in Christ Jesus our Lord" (Rom. 8:38–39).

This is the meaning of grace—approval and loving acceptance by God without having to achieve anything. It is that inner feeling of success which comes from being accepted, appreciated, and wanted by the ultimate Significant Other. For the child the word is: "When your mother and father forsake you then the Lord will take you up." For the teenager, the Good News is that Jesus is: "The Friend . . . closer than a brother." For the adult there is the question: "If Christ be for you, who can be against you?" (See Psalm 27:10; Proverbs 18:24; Romans 8:31.)

3
Successes and Sufferings of Little People

Young children generally feel successful when they sense that they have earned the approval of their parents. Sigmund Freud narrowed that to mean that children feel the most successful when they gain approval from the parent of the opposite sex. He believed that in early childhood, boys strive primarily to earn the affection and the approval of their mothers, while girls want these from their fathers.

Freud called this tendency in boys the Oedipus complex and in girls the Electra complex. Boys up to about seven to ten years of age will feel successful if they know that their mothers are proud of them. Girls in this period of development will feel successful if they know that their fathers consider them special and beautiful people.

We are aware of the limitations in much of what Freud taught, particularly his disregard of spiritual dimensions to personality. Nevertheless, his understanding of the relationships that exist between children and parents should not be overlooked; he offered valuable insights into human behavior.

Parent Approval Is Essential

As a boy I loved to hear my mother say to me, "I'm proud of you." Once I had a special part in a short play put on by our second grade class. I remember how important it was for me that my mother come to see the play and how proud I felt when she hugged me after it was over and told me that I had done so well. The achievements of Alexander the Great could not have made him feel more successful than I felt that Friday afternoon in the school auditorium. My childhood fantasies usually revolved around doing something so wonderful that I could convince my mother that she had the best and most heroic boy in the whole world.

At school or church I loved it when I had the opportunity to make things that I could take home and show her. I cannot tell you how happy I was when, after bringing home a letterholder made out of Popsicle sticks, my mother asked with apparent wonder, "Did you make this? You didn't really make this, did you?"

I remember jumping up and down with excitement and saying, "Yes I did; Yes I did! I made that and I made it for you, Mom. I made it for you." The feeling was so good that I wanted to go back and make more and better things. The feeling of success which pervaded my little body came from doing the things that gained her approval.

The Oedipus complex in boys is paralleled in girls by the Electra complex. This simply means that little girls get emotionally "hung up" on their fathers. I have interviewed many women, asking them to reflect on what made them feel successful in their early years. Each of them conveyed how important her father was in making her feel successful. One woman told me about the happiest moment in her life. As a seven-year-old girl, she played in a recital at her piano teacher's studio and her father was there proudly smiling.

Other women told about dressing up and trying to look pretty for their fathers, and how pleased they felt when their fathers paid attention to the way they looked. Each of these women had a deep childhood longing to be "daddy's little girl." They wanted their fathers to feel proud to have such talented and attractive daughters.

Parent Approval Withheld

In many cases the parents' unwillingness to give sought-for approval has had lasting and detrimental consequences in a child's future development. A friend of mine researched the lives of famous people who were noted for outstanding accomplishments. His study showed that many of them became overachievers because of the kinds of relationships they had had with parents in their earliest years.

As a case in point, imagine a little boy who strives very hard to earn his mother's approval but never feels he gains it. He works harder and harder, always hoping that if he accomplishes more she will give him what he desperately wants. She withholds approval and so he goes on pressing for higher and higher levels of achievement, hoping to win the praise of this woman who subconsciously looms as the significant other in his life.

Some boys never outgrow their felt need for the approval of their mothers. Unless children receive parental approval in the preadolescent period, they find it difficult to allow others to take the place of parents as their significant others. They become, as psychologists say, fixated in a childlike state. Throughout their lives they function as little children, ever hoping that their accomplishments will be admired by their parents.

Some parents think it is an act of love *not* to give easy approval to their children for their accomplishments. They think that by not showing early satisfaction with what their children accomplish, they will encourage them to do better. When their children proudly come home with report cards showing all *A's* except for a *B* in one subject, instead of getting applause from their parents, they are confronted with, "How come you got a *B*?"

While this tactic may motivate children to work harder in school for higher grades, it can also push them toward becoming incessant workers who are never satisfied, no matter what they achieve, and who never feel successful, no matter what other people say. My friend who researched famous people found that very few of them had a sense of satisfaction about life or any feeling of joy about what they had done. As great as their accomplishments were, these people lived with childhood impressions that they still could do better.

Encourage Your Children

In opposition to these childrearing practices, the Apostle Paul teaches us: "Fathers, do not exasperate your children; instead, bring them up in the training and instruction of the Lord" (Eph. 6:4, NIV).

Parents need this biblical admonition to keep them from pushing their children too hard and distorting their personalities. It's all right to urge children toward accomplishment, but it needs to be done in grace rather than by withholding approval and encouragement.

The way God relates to His children is the best model for encouraging children to higher levels of achievement, without inflicting emotional hurt.

1. He forgives. As He shows us how to handle our own failures, we can learn from Him how to deal with the failures and accomplishments of our children. When we fail the Lord, He not only *forgives us,* but also *justifies* us. Though it may seem childlike, I still choose to describe justification as it was explained to me when I was a boy—God treating me "just-as-if-I-never-sinned." That simple statement is a truthful portrayal of the way God handles our sins and failures: They are buried in the deepest sea and remembered no more. (See Micah 7:19.) We are told, "There is therefore now no condemnation for those who are in Christ Jesus" (Rom. 8:1). Our failures are never held against us once we have confessed them and asked for forgiveness. Parents should do the same when their children fail, by helping them to admit their failures, to learn from them, and then to leave them forgotten, where they can no longer cause depression.

Jesus not only forgets our failures, but also praises us for the good things that we do. We are told by Him that even a glass of cool water given in His name shall have its reward. (See Matthew 10:42.) In the biblical description of Judgment Day, He remembers good things that we have done even after we have forgotten, recalling that we fed the hungry, clothed the naked, and visited the sick and the captives in prison. When He reminds His people of their forgotten good deeds, they are surprised and ask, "When did we see You hungry and feed You, naked and clothe You, sick and imprisoned and visit You?"

Then Jesus will say, "Inasmuch as you have done it unto the least of these My brethren, you have done it unto Me." (See Matthew 25:34–40.)

What a Saviour! He forgets our failures, but remembers every good thing that we do and rewards us now and forever for our limited accomplishments. This is a true model of childrearing for parents everywhere!

2. *He motivates.* Jesus motivates His people to higher levels of achievement, not by withholding His symbols of love and approval, but by trying to develop a love within us that will result in service for His Kingdom. He does not try to motivate us to do the good things by promising us His love and acceptance. Instead, He surrounds us with love and acceptance, hoping that out of gratitude we will be prodded to do more and more for Him and for others. The joy that comes from the growing awareness that we *are* His and are of infinite worth, and that even our simplest good deeds have significance, motivates us to give more of ourselves for what will please Him.

As Jesus has treated us, so we should treat our children. We must accept them even when they do things which we believe to be unacceptable. When they fail we must call them to repentance but at the same time communicate to them that when they are forgiven, their failures are forgotten and not held against them. We must exalt their accomplishments and show our pride in even the little things they do for us.

Children's Reactions to Unwise Parents

1. Love-Hate. Parents who do not learn from Jesus to deal with their children in grace may create ambivalent feelings. On the one hand, their children may love them because it is the nature of most children to love their parents. But on the other hand, that love may be mixed with intense hatred and resentment for parents who make life seem impossible.

Children may also hate their parents for the feelings of inadequacy the parents have caused them to feel. This is particularly evident when parents constantly tell children that they could be doing better. This leaves the children confused about their own emotions and with ambivalent feelings toward their parents. It is enough to turn some children into neurotics.

2. Despair. Another reaction to parents who withhold enthusiastic approval of their children, regardless of their achievements, is for the children to simply give up trying to please them. Interviews with children, particularly teenagers, reveal that they often despair of ever earning praise from their parents. I remember one boy saying to me sadly, "What's the use? No matter what I do, it is never enough to please my mom and dad. I do my very best, but is that OK with them? No way! So you know what? I don't care anymore."

3. Delinquency. Sometimes resentment against overly demanding parents will result in what many social scientists call a *reaction formation*. This means that the child will do just the opposite of what the parents desire. Much delinquent behavior is the working out of resentment that children feel as a consequence of their love-hate relationship with their parents. They use delinquent acts to retaliate for their parents' failure to give them sufficient praise. The irony of this state of affairs is that very often the parents show more love and acceptance toward their children when they are delinquent than they showed when their children were trying to do what was good and right.

A typical case study of such a child might reveal a girl who tries to look pretty, get good grades in school, and be proper in her conduct, hoping to gain the adoration of her father. When he fails to appreciate her, she decides to punish him. The easiest way to do that is to become just the opposite of what he wants her to be. As she moves into her teenage years, she gives up studying, becomes sexually promiscuous, and goes out of her way to flaunt her improprieties before her father. When he tries to tell her how much she is hurting him, she subconsciously says to herself, "Good!"

The father tries to reach out to her with all kinds of expressions of affirmation and love, hoping that he can influence her for good. If only he had offered her these emotional gifts earlier, she might not ever have behaved as she did.

The Apostle Paul wrote to fathers: "Do not exasperate your children, that they may not lose heart" (Col. 3:21).

The relationships that children have with their parents dramatically color the ways these children will be able to think about God. Many social scientists argue that what children believe, think, and feel about their heavenly Father will be highly influenced by what they think about their earthly fathers. If their earthly parents seem unaccepting and disapproving, regardless of achievement, the children will come to regard their heavenly Father as unaccepting and disapproving.

Pastors often tell me how they struggle with people who seem incapable of believing that God loves and accepts them or sees infinite worth in them. These people have been conditioned, through early childhood experiences with their own parents, to view their heavenly Father as ungracious. Their pastors experience the frustration of being unable to lead them toward knowing their worth in God's sight, even after showing them verse after verse from the Scriptures about God's love and acceptance.

When I see how early childhood experiences can condition persons so that their images of God are mainly negative, I realize the miraculous nature of conversion. Only the Holy Spirit can undo emotional damage from early childhood experiences. Only a miracle can change the negative attitudes toward God generated by the bad relationships children have had with their parents.

The Miracle of Being Born Again

For several years I taught at an Ivy League university. One of my graduate students inadvertantly spoke a truth which he himself did not comprehend: "Doctor, there is no way to undo damage done by faulty social conditioning in the early stages of childhood. The hurt created by parents can never be overcome. The only hope would be if the individual would be able to go back and start over again. If somehow the individual could be born again."

I responded by saying, "But that's the Good News. Each of us can be born again." The Holy Spirit working in our lives can enable us to overcome what has been and to become what was otherwise impossible. Basic attitudinal structures can miraculously be broken down and new ones constructed. Deeply established negative images of the nature of God can be erased and new ones drawn in their place. The Scriptures teach: "If any man is in Christ he is a new creature; the old things passed away; behold, new things have come" (2 Cor. 5:17).

I cannot explain the ways in which this miracle occurs. I cannot describe the work of the Holy Spirit. But I can tell you that I have seen the impossible happen. I have seen personality structures altered and new orientations and attitudes toward God come into being.

I cannot explain the process, but I can point to the change that takes place when a person asks the resurrected Jesus, whom Christians claim is everpresent, to take possession of him, to invade his personality, to enter his psyche. Some of my fellow social scientists chide my convictions on these matters, calling them expressions of mysticism. It may be true that I am somewhat mystical; but to the scientifically minded, I can say that the results of surrendering to Jesus are empirically verifiable.

Children Want to Please Their Parents

The tendency for children to work intensely to please their parents can easily be exploited. I have to wonder how many children have been baptized or confirmed into the membership of the church because of a deep desire to please their parents. I know that when I was a pastor there were many children who came to me asking for baptism primarily for this reason. I am convinced that many people have become missionaries or pastors for wrong reasons. In early childhood they learned that if they went into these church vocations, their parents would be very proud.

During the time I was host of a talk show on a Philadelphia television station, my fifteen-year-old son was a guest on my show. One day I asked him if he felt I had ever pressured him in the selection of a life's vocation. He replied, "Not directly. No matter what I mention as a possible career you say, 'OK that's nice.' But if I say I'm thinking of becoming a minister, you light up and go bananas."

I hope and pray that if my son ever decides to be a minister, his motivation will be something other than a desire to gain my approval.

Since children are anxious to please, parents must be very careful of this kind of manipulation. When children do right things for wrong reasons, they may suffer confusion and resentment when they are grown. As young adults develop the capacity to reflect upon the motivations behind their youthful decisions, they sometimes deliberately reverse those decisions. For instance, if they realize that their basic reason for choosing to be baptized or joining the church was because of manipulation by their parents, they may become resentful and reject Christianity altogether.

These grown children may not only reject the God that their

parents manipulated them into accepting, but also the manipulators themselves. They may become angry with their parents and estranged from them when the children realize that their own desire to please was exploited unfairly.

On the other hand, we must admit that there are more people whose desire to please their parents led them to seriously consider Christ and accept Him as Saviour, without negative effects. When children sense that Jesus is important to their parents, they may become genuinely open to the Gospel in a rich and meaningful way.

Parents need to communicate to their children that they are accepted and loved whether they accept Christ as personal Saviour or not. Acceptance of Christ should not be a condition for gaining parental approval.

Comparison Can Be Abusive

One of the worst abuses by parents is trying to elicit great accomplishments from children by comparing them with their brothers and sisters or with children from outside the family. The mother who says, "Why can't you be like your sister?" may be responsible for setting brother and sister against each other in such a way that they can never enjoy one another. Such children may never feel successful unless they are outdoing their brothers and sisters. How sad it is to see parents stimulate rivalry between their own children so that family solidarity is lost, love is diminished, and even hatred comes into play.

Parents should be committed to making each child feel that he or she is appreciated in a special way. Parents should be affirming the uniqueness of each child rather than exploiting comparisons. To be a truly Christian parent is to be sensitive to those traits which make each child special, and to show appreciation for that uniqueness.

4
School Daze

When children enter school, important transitions occur in their lives. One of the most important is when the children begin to regard the recognition granted by teachers to be as important as that granted by parents. Whereas being successful formerly meant approval from parents, children in school begin to treat approval from their teachers with equal importance. To many children teachers become glorious, all knowing, all-powerful creatures. Receiving positive feedback from these teachers affirms the children in almost miraculous ways. Likewise, some children who feel put down or unappreciated by their teachers develop very poor self-images which may result in inferiority complexes that torture them for the rest of their lives.

My wife has told me many times about the influence her seventh-grade teacher had on her. He was handsome, intelligent, kind, and seemed almost godlike. Pleasing him became the primary motivation of her life. She did her homework with great dedication and was thrilled every time a paper was returned with an A on it. Having the teacher praise her work gave her a sense of success about life that no one could challenge.

I remember my fifth-grade teacher. She loved me and delighted in my accomplishments. This made me want to do more and more good work for her. I wished this wonderful lady were my age so that we could grow up together and be married. Nothing could have seemed better than to spend the rest of my life with this most significant person. For me there was no question but that success lay in doing things she thought were worthwhile, and doing them in a way that she would applaud.

Why was she so special? She was the first teacher who made me feel that she really believed in me, and so helped me to believe in myself. She was the first one who saw me as a success in academic work. I wonder if I would be a college teacher today if Miss Barr had not shown me the success I could feel through academic accomplishments.

Teachers as Significant Others

Any parent knows how important teachers are to children. What teachers say often is more important than what parents say. Teachers can become the ultimate source of truth. I remember when arguments with my daughter would conclude with her haughty assertion that I was wrong because what I said differed with what her teacher had said. When the words, ''My teacher told me'' prefaced her statements, I knew there was no point in disputing them. The teacher had replaced me as the significant other in her life.

One of the amusing events in rearing my daughter was the time when she discovered that one of her teachers had been my student in graduate school. The idea that her father could be her teacher's teacher was hard for her to handle, and I know that I went up in her estimation because her teacher respected my opinions.

Lack of Recognition

The role of the teacher as the significant other for the growing child has potential for both good and evil. We have cited ways in which children can become more successful students if they have teachers who believe in them and praise their accomplishments. However, there are cases in which teachers have failed their students by withholding appreciation and praise when children have made efforts to earn these responses. After my daughter had turned in a science project on which she had spent many hours, she told me in a discouraged manner, "You know, it really didn't make any difference at all that I did that work. The teacher didn't think what I made was special at all."

A friend of mine is an angry leader in the Chicano communities of the Southwest. His most intense anger is over what he says the Anglo schoolteachers are doing to Latino children. He tells me that many of the teachers do not expect Mexican-American children to accomplish much, and consequently, they don't. These teachers do not give recognition to the efforts made by Chicano children when they try to learn, and the children come away from their classes with no sense of accomplishment. My friend claims that if these children are to feel successful, they must have teachers who believe in them and expect them to learn. If the children cannot be made to feel successful in school, they will want to drop out to get away from those who foster their feelings of insignificance.

As a sociologist, I am convinced that feeling like a failure at school is a major cause of juvenile delinquency. Children retreat from classrooms and from teachers who make them feel unsuccessful, and look for some other group that will give them more positive feelings. The youngster who is willing to do something daringly antisocial can gain instantaneous praise from the gang that hangs out on the street corner. If being foulmouthed, tough, and defiant are traits which the gang will praise, children craving for approval will quickly acquire them.

A Child's Self-Image

Parents need to be very concerned about the effects that teachers are having on their children. Parents cannot assume that school experiences are going well simply because children are getting good grades and seem to be mastering their academic assignments. School is much more than reading, writing, and arithmetic. Perhaps the most important thing that any child can receive from the years spent in school is a positive self-image that leaves him convinced of his personal worth.

Parents should not be deterred from interfering in any teacher-child relationship that seems to be having a detrimental effect on the child. Children are far too precious for their self-images to be distorted. If little can be done to alter the negative effects that a teacher is having on a child, then the parents should consider having that child removed to another classroom where the effects of teacher-child interaction will be more positive. If need be, the child may have to move to a different school. This might cost money, but I question the value system of the family that is willing to spend thousands for a new automobile but unwilling to invest in the development of their children.

Too often, parents think that it is best not to interfere in school situations, even when they are alarmed by what is happening to their child. They have heard other parents suggest that it is good for the child to struggle through a negative teacher-child arrangement, even if it leaves the child depressed about himself and antagonistic about school. Nothing could be further from the truth.

Parents and children have the right to expect the school to provide teachers who affirm pupils, enable them to believe in themselves, and give them feelings of positive achievement. When this right is denied, the parents must see the principal or school counselor in order to change the situation. If they allow the child to try to resolve such a problem for himself, it could be too much for him to handle, and the influence of the teacher too great for the child to overcome.

Usually the other members of the child's class will come to view him through the teacher's eyes. The opinion of the teacher is so highly respected by most students that when the teacher defines a child as a failure in some way, the other pupils in the class reinforce that judgment, and provide such a negative social environment for the child that coping becomes impossible.

How Are Your Children Taught?

In analyzing how school experiences influence children to feel like successes or failures, we must pay attention not only to the role of teachers, but also to the very processes by which education is carried out.

Marshall McLuhan has said, "The medium is the message." The *way* children are taught communicates messages of far greater importance than *what* they are taught. Let me illustrate what I mean.

When I was 10 years old, I regularly walked to school with my good friend Albert, who was the smartest boy in the class. One particular day Albert and I walked to school together, went into our classroom, and took our seats as usual. The teacher started class by giving us good news. "Today we're going to play a game."

I was thrilled. I hated school and loved games. The idea of playing instead of studying made me happy.

She said, "Boys and girls, we're going to play baseball." This was almost too much. I loved baseball. Then she said, "We're going to play spelling baseball."

The second announcement deflated me. I hated spelling. As the child of an Italian immigrant family, I found spelling impossible, and not because I was stupid. Any language that spells pneumonia with a "p" has to be devoid of rationality.

The teacher chose captains for the two teams. Naturally, Albert was chosen. The other team captain was a girl named Mary. I couldn't stand Mary; she was one of those perfect children who did everything just right. She dressed right, she spoke right, she walked right, and she smiled right. She was constantly held up before us as a shining example of what we were supposed to be. I don't know how many times children in our class were put down with the statement, "Why can't you be good like Mary?"

The captains were allowed to pick their team members. I sat there feeling "cool" because Albert was my friend and I assumed that he would pick me first. I was wrong; Albert did not pick me first. He did not pick me second. He did not pick me third. I began to wave my hand in his face in the frantic style that is characteristic of grade-school children who want to be chosen. Still Albert did not choose me. He seemed to look right through me and went on selecting other children.

I was shaken but I *was* learning. What I was learning was that in this game, friendship did not count. The only thing that counted was how successfully a child could spell. It was then and there that I learned that, within this competitive system, success was more important than friendship. Acceptance and rejection depended upon success, and success alone.

The teacher didn't understand when three weeks later she caught me cheating in a spelling test. She said to me, "Tony, don't you know you can't learn how to spell by copying the answers off someone else's paper?" Foolish teacher! Didn't she know that I didn't care about spelling? All I cared about was the evidence of success that would earn me the acceptance of my peers.

The selection of team members continued and still I was left behind. Albert had forsaken me. Finally, there were only two of us not chosen—just me and another kid who went to a special school the next year. Even then, Albert didn't want me. But I was assigned to his team.

As I stood glued against the wall of the classroom staring at the opposing team, I waited nervously for my turn, dreading it as it drew near. I failed on the first word I was asked to spell, *grasshopper*. I didn't know the word had two *Ps*. The teacher's words were painful to hear: "You're out. Now take your seat."

No one in the world can feel more alone than the first one out in spelling baseball. As I crawled to my seat, all the members of my team booed me, and to make my humiliation complete, the members of the opposing team cheered my failure. As I tried to disappear under my desk by slumping as low as possible, my only hope was that others would fail too; then I would not be the only one out. People who fail always feel like that. Failure is a little less torturous if there are others who share it with you.

The teacher turned to the other team and asked, "Does anyone here know how to spell *grasshopper?*"

Little Mary knew. I can still see and hear her. "Grasshopper," she said (in such a prissy manner). "G-R-A-S-S-H-O-P-P-E-R." With each letter she swung her shoulders, and as each letter sounded, it was like a knife being stabbed into my stomach. I felt like I was dying.

My Failure Means Your Success

I was learning a lesson that had nothing to do with spelling. The lesson was this: Mary's success was built on my failure; my failure was a condition for Mary's triumph. This is the lesson that prepares the individual to live in our kind of world. Businessmen who have learned it well can delight in the failure of their competitors, knowing that those failures are their own opportunities to succeed. Some people may even long for the failures of their closest friends.

This is one place where a dominant American value runs contrary to the values inherent in Scripture. The Apostle Paul warns us against such feelings when he tells us in 1 Corinthians 13 that the loving Christian rejoices not in the failures but in the successes of others.

It is a cop-out to shrug our shoulders and say, "That's the system. You've got to learn to live with it." We *don't* have to.

Existentialist Jean Paul Sartre spoke against this human tendency to accept the structures of society as though they were invulnerable to change. He called this "bad faith."

God wants us to struggle against "the principalities and powers" that lessen our humanity. I believe this means that when a social practice diminishes an individual's self-worth, that practice must be challenged by the people of God.

I am convinced that most children who hate school feel that way because the educational system makes them feel like failures. Most children love discovering and exploring what is new, and they are thrilled when their perception of the world is expanded. Learning new things makes them feel wonderfully grown-up.

Very often parents will say to me, "I know my child is intelligent. He has a good head on his shoulders, but he doesn't want to work. He just won't do his homework. I know that he could do well in school if he would just try. Tell me, Dr. Campolo, why doesn't he want to study?"

Take a good look at the system. Your child may be refusing to study because he doesn't want to be a part of a system that refuses to affirm him as a person or give him positive feelings of self-worth. His only way of rebelling against the system is noncooperation. For many children school is agony.

Grandiose Dreams

Some children cope with their present feelings of failure by convincing themselves that they will someday be famous and achieve such great things, that they will be admired far and wide, particularly by those who scorn them in the present. Unfortunately, their dreams are usually grandiose beyond any possibility of coming true. Most of these children will always feel like failures.

The Bible teaches us that "young men shall see visions" and "old men shall dream dreams" (Acts 2:17). When this is not the case, the Scriptures tell us that the people perish. (See Proverbs 29:18.) Christians should challenge an educational system that so fills children with a sense of failure that they escape into an unrealistic world of fantasies.

One of the saddest discussions I've ever had was with a 14-year-old black student who had been raised in the ghetto and denied a valid education. He could hardly read at the third-grade level. His teacher viewed him as hopeless and his classmates considered him stupid. Nevertheless, when I spoke with him, he told me that when he grew up he was going to be the "best and most famous brain surgeon in the world."

I don't think that it is racist to suggest that this youngster had unrealistic dreams. I understood why he had them. He seemed to be saying to me, and to himself, "Someday I'll show them! They might laugh at me now, but someday I'll be so famous that they will be proud to have known me!"

No matter what this young man achieves in life, I think he will feel like a failure. He will experience the frustration that comes to a person who lacks the means to realize his goals. As his hurt turns to anger, who knows how he will try to get back at a world that has caused him so much pain?

Parochial Schools?

When we consider what the normative educational process does to children in the public school system, we are prone to ask whether it might not be better to have children educated in Christian parochial schools. Over the past decade, hundreds of such institutions have sprung up across the nation, offering us an alternative to the secular educational system which communicates the dominant values of the culture rather than the values inherent in the Christian Gospel.

These schools seemed to hold great promise for delivering children from the destructive competition so characteristic of public schools. Many of us assumed that Christian schools would veer away from those teaching techniques which have created negative self-images and feelings of personal failure for so many children. We thought that the Christian day school would allow children to be educated in a context that affirmed individual worth. We believed that children would not be pitted against each other in ways that created emotional alienation. We supposed the expectation, that all children in a given age bracket should be able to accomplish the same things, would be discarded. But for the most part, our hopes have not been realized.

In the best of Christian day schools, an attempt is made to

integrate Christian teachings into the curriculum. Usually, biology is taught so that children see how God was involved in the development of life. Art and music teach the tremendous contributions of the people of God. History courses take into account the greatest event in the annals of recorded time—the life of Christ. Special chapel programs in Christian schools present the Gospel story and the theology of the church. But while the content of the educational process may be Christian, the way in which the children are taught is usually the same as in the public school system.

An Ideal Christian School

What I long to see is the establishment of more Christian schools where the goals include not only communication of the message of Jesus, the accumulated knowledge of the society, and the development of the individual talents of the students, but also *an educational process that gives children feelings of deep personal worth, an awareness of their accomplishments, and feelings of success.* Such schools would shy away from standardized expectations for all children, recognizing, as Jesus does, that each child has unique gifts, traits, and abilities, and will develop at a rate different from his peers.

In such a school each child would be evaluated in terms of how well he was realizing his own potential, rather than how he compared to others at the same age level. Success would no longer be dependent upon competitive comparisons, but rather on the degree to which the child was discovering and developing the gifts that God had given him.

A Kibbutz School

A close approximation of the system being advocated has been developed in the State of Israel. The Jewish people have created a model for education that is worthy of some consideration by those of us trying to implement Christian principles into the educational process. I am, of course, referring to the Israeli kibbutz (a communal farm). As this system is analyzed, I must enter a disclaimer: I am not advocating this system, only asking that we study some of its educational principles.

In one kibbutz I studied, the whole emphasis was to build a high level of solidarity among members and to work for the emotional adjustment of each child. The medium of education was designed to reach these goals. In the morning when the children arrived at school, they were expected to put on uniforms. The interesting thing about these uniforms was that the buttons were arranged in the back of the clothes, leaving the children in the strange predicament of not being able to fasten them by themselves. Each child had to depend on another student to help him dress and prepare for the experiences of the day. This was just one subtle means whereby children were taught to depend upon each other in a cooperative and helpful manner, rather than to view one another as competitors.

Another way that this kibbutz encouraged mutuality and interdependence was through play. All children enjoy building things with wooden blocks. However, in this kibbutz, the blocks were so heavy that a single child could not lift any of them. For the child to build anything, he would have to cooperate with one or two other children. By working together they could achieve what no one of them could alone.

Of particular interest to me was the educational process in the upper grades. There the students progressed only as fast as the slowest child could learn. When a test was given and one of the students failed, the class would then go back over the material until that student could successfully complete the examination. It was interesting to see how the other children in the class helped the slow student along in his studies. They had a vested interest in the slow student's accomplishments. They could not learn additional material until the material already taught was mastered by their slower friend. So they encouraged him and cheered his every accomplishment, and when he finally did comprehend the material, they made him feel that he had done something wonderful for all of them—and indeed he had.

This concern for the slower student is quite a contrast to the contempt that fast learners often show within our highly competitive learning system. If, as a slow student in spelling, I had been surrounded by encouragement and support from my peers instead of the put-down that I experienced from Mary and the others while playing spelling baseball, my whole self-concept might be different today.

This is not to suggest that the style of education in a kibbutz is problem-free. Bruno Bettelheim, one of America's leading psychologists, made careful studies of life in the kibbutz. He found that while it did much to diminish neurotic drives toward achievement and to help children gain a better acceptance of themselves as persons, the system left much to be desired. For instance, Bettelheim pointed out that young people in the kibbutz often lacked the capability to make individualistic decisions; they lacked autonomy and often did not know how to function when each member was left on his own. Furthermore, Bettelheim discovered that the children of the kibbutz lacked long-range goals in life. They were so devoid of a drive for achievement that they seldom saw success as a goal for which present sacrifices should be made.

Competition is part of the real world in which children must eventually function. Long-range goals are necessary. Undoubtedly, the kibbutz would not adequately prepare people to function in modern America. Nevertheless, efforts must be made to deliver children from the kind of destructive competition that is dehumanizing.

If God has given us children to raise in the nurture and admonition of the Lord, we should be committed to developing all of the gifts within each child. Children need to see that in the competitive struggles which are part of school and play, the most important goal should be to surpass one's own previous achievements rather than to prove superiority over peers. We can help children love themselves because they sense their infinite worth and not because they do better than other children. Only those who love themselves properly can truly love Christ and other people. Developing this capacity in children is essential for the future of the nation and of the world.

5
Coming
of Age
in America

As a child moves into the teenage years, he feels an increasing need to be popular. In fact, there is a great likelihood that popularity will become his ultimate goal.

To achieve this, the teenager in our modern culture develops what sociologist David Reisman calls an *other-directed personality*. He develops a sixth sense which enables him to pick up from any group what they expect from him. Once he has a reading on the group, he is able to conform to what he believes will gain him group approval.

It is fascinating to watch a teenager come into a new group. At first he simply observes, attempting not to reveal any of his own thoughts or feelings. He "plays it cool," trying to communicate an air of detachment. Because he is careful not to respond with either enthusiasm or contempt to what the other members of the group are doing, his face may appear almost emotionless. He is "playing it cool" to allow himself time to figure out what the members of the group expect him to be. Once he has "the feel" of the group, he will gradually begin to behave in ways which he believes will earn him approval and acceptance.

It takes a long time to develop this sixth sense. Some young people never do and consequently, may be labeled as *weird, klutz,* and *nerd*. There seems to be no end to the labels young people dream up for those individuals who miscalculate what the group expects of them, and do and say the wrong things with the wrong people. When a particular young person is guilty of this "unforgiveable sin," his peers usually say that he has "blown it." The horrible thing is that once the individual has blown it, there is not much he can do to set things right. Teenagers are very unforgiving; once they have defined an individual as a loser, he might just as well give up, or try to achieve success with another group somewhere else.

Other-directed Teens

Adult advisers who work with church youth groups need to remember that the behavior of teenagers tends to be *other-directed*. When a young person comes to the meeting and sits there seemingly detached, emotionless, and even sullen, the youth leader may ask himself, "Why does he come if he's not going to get anything out of it?" He comes because he wants to be accepted by the members of the group and to gain popularity in their eyes. He sits there looking detached and uninvolved because he hasn't yet figured out what will earn him that treasured approval.

At one time when I was the leader of a church youth group, I became very frustrated because my group wouldn't sing choruses that had always been such an enjoyment to me when I was their age. I was further perplexed because when I would take them to a youth rally where there were hundreds of other young people, they would then sing their lungs out. I'd ask myself, "Why can't I get them to sing like that?"

The answer is that they sang with enthusiasm at the youth rally because they sensed that it was expected of them; they failed to sing at the small youth gathering because they were afraid they would look ridiculous in the eyes of their peers.

Group Acceptance

Adults too easily forget how disastrous it is when a young person blows his chances for group acceptance. Should it take place in a church gathering, there is a strong probability that the young person will never come back to the church again. When this happens at the high school, the student may not only withdraw from school activities, but may also long to move to a new town where he can start over again and have another chance at gaining acceptance by the "in" crowd.

On occasion, I have seen rejection by the "in" group at school result in tremendous dedication to the church. A young person who fails to "make it" with the gang at school may become intensely committed to the church youth group if he finds a community of acceptance there that makes him feel worthwhile. Many a young person has come to Christ for that reason alone.

I do not want to question commitments to the church that are made on such grounds, but I would offer a reminder that involvement in the church youth group does not necessarily mean that the individual is committed to Christ. The two sometimes go together, but not always.

The church has always attracted society's losers because they can feel like winners within its fellowship. The early church grew because many people who were rejects in society found acceptance and affirmation within the community of believers.

But Christianity must go deeper than group affirmation if it is to be genuine. It must involve a person's relationship with the resurrected Christ. Because such a relationship is often communicated through a loving group, it is possible for an individual to love the church fellowship without loving Jesus.

The Chameleon

It is easy for the other-directed personality to be superficial. His behavior is not so much determined by inner conviction as it is by what other people expect. In each group he gets a reading of what is expected of him and accordingly conforms. These groups may have values and expectations that are vastly different from each other, but the completely other-directed person will be able to succeed in all of them. He simply alters his personality as he moves from group to group, so that with one set of associates he is one kind of person, while with another group he becomes entirely different.

For several years I was a faculty proctor, living in the men's dormitory of a small Christian liberal arts college, where I got to know my students very well. One particular young man seemed to lack any semblance of Christian commitment. He had no time for the church or for the Bible study groups on campus, and he ridiculed those who took such things seriously. He often went drinking with friends at the local bar, and was sexually pro-miscuous.

One evening after I had spoken at a church, a middle-aged woman came to me and asked if I knew her son who was a student at my college. I knew him all right—he was the very boy I have just described. The woman then went on to say, "Isn't he a lovely boy? He is such a deeply committed Christian. When he's home during the summer, he is a leader of the youth here at church. He conducts the Bible study at the midweek service when the pastor is away on vacation. Everyone at the church looks up to him and thinks I'm so lucky to have such a wonderful son."

I immediately began to wonder if her boy and the young man I knew at college were one and the same person. The answer was Yes. He was other-directed. When he was home with the church people, his behavior was "churchy," and when he was away at school, he sought the approval of a group with different values.

The German existentialist writer, Martin Heidegger, would have called him *inauthentic*. Jean Paul Sartre would have said he was *guilty of nonbeing*.

We will simply call him an expression of David Reisman's other-directed personality. Here was a young man who lacked any personal identity. By the end of each day, he had played so many different roles for so many different groups that he could legitimately look in the mirror and ask himself, "Will the real me please step forward?"

When I returned to school, I met this young man in the hallway of our classroom building, and said, "Guess where I was last night? I was at the Lakeview Baptist Church."

He said, "That's my church!" I replied, "I know, and Charlie, we both know what a phony you are. You're a completely different person at home with those church people, aren't you?" His head dropped, and shame seemed to overwhelm him.

The following semester Charlie came straight to my office and said, "Dr. Campolo, remember that talk we had last year in the hallway? Well, you were right; I was being phony. But it's different now. I want you to know that this summer I never attended church once."

That wasn't exactly what I had in mind, but I would have to say that the young man was then closer to the kingdom of God than ever before. At least he knew that Christianity is not a style of behavior one assumes when he is with Christian people, that it is more than saying the right words and doing the right things in the right setting. He had come to grips with what Christianity is not, and this might set him up for a confrontation with what Christianity is—a personal surrender to Jesus who guides from within, no matter where you are.

I am happy to report that I was able to lead this young man to a knowledge of Jesus Christ as Lord and Saviour, and that he is now living what I believe to be a consistent life for Christ. Many times I have thanked God for the opportunity to confront him with the incongruities of his life.

Need for Individuality

Young people are aware of their tendencies to conform to the expectations of others. Many of them, deep down inside, condemn such conformity and crave to be individuals with the integrity to stand up to any group and to affirm their identity, regardless of what others might think. But they don't know how to be individualistic. Even in their attempts at nonconformity, they seem to be imitating others. The members of the rebellious youth culture often look alike, dress alike, and talk alike. Even in their rebellion, they are conforming to what they think will gain them acceptance with their counterculture friends.

Young people need to see that social nonconformity has its most positive expression in becoming a Christian and being guided from within by the Holy Spirit. The Apostle Paul wrote: "I urge you therefore, brethren, by the mercies of God, to present your bodies a living and holy sacrifice, acceptable to God, which is your spiritual service of worship. And do not be conformed to this world, but be transformed by the renewing of your mind, that you may prove what the will of God is, that which is good and acceptable and perfect" (Rom. 12:1–2).

Or, as J.B. Phillips translates these verses: "With eyes wide open to the mercies of God, I beg you, my brothers, as an act of intelligent worship, to give Him your bodies, as a living sacrifice, consecrated to Him and acceptable by Him. Don't let the world around you squeeze you into its own mold, but let God remold your minds from within, so that you may prove in practice that the plan of God for you is good, meets all His demands, and moves toward the goal of true maturity."

Young people need to understand that if they invite Jesus into their lives, the influence He will exert on their behavior from within will be greater than that exerted on them by the expectations of others. In Christ is the source of true individuality.

6
Teenage Success
with the
Opposite Sex

Success for young people is tied to gaining the approval of their peers. And of all the members of their peer groups, those of the opposite sex loom as the most significant. Most boys want to be approved by girls, and girls want to gain recognition from the boys.

Popularity with the opposite sex can make young people feel that they have achieved what is most important in life. Also, they are seen as successful in the eyes of their peers. This means that the boy who is successful with girls will be admired by his male companions, and the girl who is successful with the boys will gain admiration from her female friends.

The boy who can date the most sought-after girls has achieved the ultimate status symbol in the youth subculture. The girl who has so many boys chasing her that she has to beat them off is the envy of most other girls. She finds that even her parents take pride in her popularity with boys. The importance of dating in the teenage culture cannot be exaggerated. The dating game is played for stakes that are too high for most of us older folks to remember very well.

The Teenage Boy

There are several marks of success—as seen by a teenage boy.

1. Humor. The adolescent male is convinced that to be successful with girls he must have a good personality. In the teenage subculture that means "being funny." He will try hard to be funny and to entertain everyone with his jokes. Unfortunately, it takes years to become witty and to develop sophisticated humor. This means that the average teenager often ends up making a fool of himself. Sometimes he tells bad jokes which inflict pain on others. Being funny is so important that he might even try to get a cheap laugh by ridiculing someone who seems to be a bit weird to his crowd. If all else fails, an off-color joke can be used to get the gang laughing. He knows that most of his friends are afraid not to laugh at dirty jokes for fear that they will be considered immature. And what could be worse for a teenager than to have his friends consider him immature?

I am not trying to excuse any of this behavior. Rather I want you to understand it and have some pity for the boy who is trying too hard to be funny. Youth leaders need to be prepared for the struggling teenager who continuously disrupts the meetings with inane remarks.

When I was 16, being funny was so important that I seldom gave consideration to how my "humor" affected others. One of the "funny" things my friends and I did was associated with driving our buddy Billy Turner home after a basketball game. It would be about midnight when we drove up to his row home. As he got out of the car, we would honk the horn and scream at the top of our lungs, "Hey, Mrs. Turner, here comes your drunken son." The driver then would step on the gas, spin his wheels, and with the screech of spinning rubber we would zoom away. By this time, Billy Turner's neighbors would be awake and his parents angry. We all thought this was very funny.

The practical joker who gets a laugh at another person's expense is omnipresent in the teenage world. He may pull out the chair behind you as you sit down, or loosen the lids on the salt shakers in the cafeteria; he has an endless array of such tricks. Being funny is his way to popularity.

2. *Possessions.* Another route taken by teenage boys seeking status—and girls too—is purchasing the right consumer goods. Jules Henry, the famous anthropologist, has pointed out that we live in a consumer society where one gains status by possessing the right things. A boy thinks if he wears the right clothes, drives the right car, listens to the right kind of records, and plays them on the right kind of stereo, people will think he's "really with it."

Possessing the right things *does* gain some status in the youth subculture, and young people know it. Parents find themselves constantly being nagged by their children, who seem to have an unending list of things that cost too much money. Although parents get exasperated over these materialistic demands, they should understand that their children want these things in order to gain the acceptance that possessing them may bring.

3. *Sports.* Another way for males to achieve popularity in the youth culture is through sports. I remember being willing to do almost anything in my teenage years to make the varsity basketball team. I knew that being on the team would gain me instant status with males and females alike. For endless hours I practiced my jump shot, constantly fantasizing about scoring the winning basket for my school against its arch rival. The scene was always the same: I saw myself stealing the ball and shooting a jump shot from at least 20 feet out, while the crowd roared in excitement and the final gun went off, just as the ball swished through the net. I imagined a voice, like Howard Cosell's, broadcasting in the background, "Campolo steals the ball, dribbles to the top of the key—leaps into the air—he lets go of the jump shot—IT'S GOOD!"

In my fantasy this was always followed by the roar of the crowd. But most important of all was that the girls, including that special girl, were impressed.

Sports can be valuable, but not when they become the primary means in a struggle for popularity. We kid ourselves into thinking that it is just good clean body-building and sportsmanship that are being developed in high school athletics. A great deal of what goes on in the name of sports is an attempt for males to gain recognition, particularly from females. There is nothing wrong with popularity, but there is something wrong when all of a youth's activities are aimed at achieving that one goal.

4. *Talking big.* Having the right things, making the team, pulling off the right stunts mean very little unless the "right" people know about them. Consequently, every boy must master the technique of letting other people know about him without seeming like a braggart. As a young person, I particularly liked those occasions when I was away from home for the summer vacation. If I was at a camp 100 miles from home, I felt that I had an opportunity to gain status simply by "talking big." I exaggerated my limited athletic accomplishments until I was a superstar. I would talk of what I owned, places I had been, and things I had done. And I did so with a style that I believed would convince them I was incredibly wonderful. I remember being afraid that someone might learn the truth about me. I never wanted any of them to visit me when camp was over lest they learn the reality that I was just an ordinary kid. Sometimes I shuddered at the thought of being found out.

The tendency to exaggerate exploits in order to build an image bigger than life is characteristic of most boys, but it is never more evident than in those crucial teenage years when gaining popularity with one's peers—and particularly the girls—is of ultimate importance. Young people often feel guilty over these deceptions and are afraid that they will be found out. By exaggerating, the young person is really suggesting that he is not worthy to be liked as he is and must appear to be something different in order to be popular. This behavior is evidence of self-rejection. If only he could be more than he is!

The Teenage Girl

The need to be successful at dating is even more urgent for girls than for boys. Many girls feel as if they are nothing if they fail to attract the kind of dates they desperately want. However, a girl faces special problems because of society's demands.

1. Good looks for self-esteem. For the female trying to succeed at the dating game, the most important attribute is "good looks." It won't do to tell the teenage girl that "looks aren't everything." She knows better. She realizes that boys don't pay much attention to those who are physically unattractive. She knows that girls who are unattractive are referred to as "dogs" by the boys. One consequence of living in a sexist society is that a female may have personality, depth of character, wit, intelligence, and untold positive traits, but she doesn't stand much of a chance without an attractive face and a well-shaped body.

The female who fails to measure up to the appearance prescribed by society often finds that not even her family will provide her with a positive self-image. Parents tend to view their children as they think other teenagers see them. I have seen mothers brag about their daughters by pointing out the fact that their daughters have more dates than they can handle. Some mothers believe that their daughters are beautiful if they get a lot of dates, and I have known mothers who define their daughters as unattractive because those girls are ignored by the boys.

One summer when I was teaching at the University of Pennsylvania, a very attractive woman came into class and took her place in the front row. By any definition she would have to be described as stunning. In fact, she was so attractive that her very presence became a distraction in my small class. The students and I usually had lunch together and we got to know each other quite well. In the course of our many discussions, it became obvious that this young woman had a very low self-concept. She didn't believe herself to be worth anything and seemed to have no idea how beautiful she was.

We couldn't understand the source of her low self-esteem until one day she passed around some high school photographs. Suddenly we understood. In high school she had been plump, her dress and her hairstyle had been out of fashion and she had looked very plain. She had probably been dateless and had developed a very negative self-image. In her early 20s her body had shaped into what this culture calls attractive. She had learned how to dress fashionably, and her face had matured into beauty; but it was too late. She was stuck with an earlier self-image that would not change, in spite of what she had become.

A few years later, while in Manhattan, I stepped into a bar just off Times Square looking for a telephone. There, sitting on a bar stool looking for a pick-up, was my former student. My heart sank and I turned away so as not to embarrass her by my recognition. She is just one example of what can happen to those girls who lose out with the boys in high school. The system made my student feel worthless and she behaved in ways that reflected a poor self-image.

2. *The trauma of school dances.* The emotional brutality that females must endure in the dating game became clear to me when I was still in high school. During my senior year I was elected president of the student council. That was a real ego trip and everyone was happy for me. The pastor of my church patted me on the back and told me that this was an opportunity to be "a real testimony for Jesus." (I have never understood why the church thinks that those who are socially successful have the testimonies most worth hearing. The Lord does equally exciting work among those whom the world rejects.)

To my surprise, I discovered that one of my responsibilities as student council president was to set up a dance for the student body each month. My problem was that I belonged to one of those churches which taught that dancing was wrong. My pastor said, "It stimulates the lust of the flesh." There is undoubtedly truth to what he said, as any observation of a disco dance will support, but I doubt that what goes on at most school dances is any worse than what goes on at most church hayrides.

In any event, I resolved the dilemma of fulfilling my responsibilities as student council president, while remaining faithful to the expectations of my church, by setting up the dance, being present when it took place, but *not* dancing. This afforded me a detachment from the dance that allowed me to observe what was going on.

The decorating committee and I got to the school gym about 6:30 in the evening. We opened the windows to air out the place because the basketball team had just finished practicing. Next we got out the crepe paper which was always used to decorate for such occasions, and strung it across the room.

At 7:00 Roger showed up. I was surprised to see him because he wasn't the kind of boy I thought would have much success with the girls in such a setting. He was a bit "whifty" and had not developed those other-directed traits that would have enabled him to fit in with his peers. He was strange, awkward, and lanky. Under Roger's right arm were records and I immediately knew what he was going to do. All evening he would be the one who would sit up on the stage changing records and keeping the music going so others could dance.

Playing the records was Roger's way of participating in the dance without getting hurt, and yet he was hurting. I knew he was hurting. When the teacher who was serving as a chaperone told me that she thought everyone was having a good time, I was positive that she had not given proper consideration to poor Roger.

Around the four walls of the gym, we arranged folding chairs. That evening about 50 girls were sitting on them with bored looks of indifference. I watched them as they put on an air of sophistication and pretended that they were really above what was happening on the dance floor. But their facade of nonchalance was only an attempt to cover up the anxieties and fears they had, as they sat there wondering whether or not they would be asked to dance.

They were hoping with all their might that they would not end up as total rejects. They suffered in quiet desperation but knew that they dared not show it.

After the dance was over, I was standing out on 48th Street in front of West Philadelphia High, when my lab partner came running out of the school. She was a special girl, undoubtedly the wittiest person I knew. Besides that, she had a kindness and sweetness about her that made her a joy to all who knew her. As she ran by me I yelled in my friendliest manner, "Hi!"

She didn't answer and that was so unlike her. She jumped into a waiting automobile and before her father could drive her away from the curb, I watched my friend Mary break down and cry. I felt angry with the whole scene and decided then and there that I would never take part in another school dance.

My opposition to dances did not stem from the belief that relates to the lust of the flesh. Instead, it stemmed from the hurt that I saw so many endure.

3. *Perennial rejects.* I have only been describing the hurt experienced by those who came to the dance. I cannot imagine what it was like for the greater proportion of the student body who stayed home that evening because they knew what would happen if they came. They did not want to subject themselves to that kind of possible rejection. How hard it must have been for them when their mothers asked, "Why don't you go to the dance tonight and have a good time?"

What does one answer? "I'm a reject"? "I'm a loser"? "I'm a nothing"?

Perhaps a well-meaning father will "drive the final nails into the coffin" as he says in love, "I know—let's all go out together this evening."

It is no wonder that the teenager often answers angrily, "Why don't you leave me alone?"

Of course, dating is not destructive for everyone. There are many young people who go out and have good times. However, even for them I have a warning. The dating game as a whole, and the dance in particular, are deceiving. The dating game leads people to think that the traits which make them successful in these activities are the ones that really matter in life. The truth is that these traits don't matter very much in the adult world.

Few things are as pathetic as watching a middle-aged woman trying to look and act like a teenager. As she senses that the traits that made her successful in those earlier days are slipping away, she tries desperately to hold onto them. She doesn't dress or act her age because she feels so threatened by having lost those attributes which made her the queen at the senior prom. Most of the traits which make for success in dating will not help much in real life.

A university student, after hearing one of my lectures condemning the dating game, gave me this poem.

Ode To A Pretty Girl

Pretty girl
when you walk by
our eyes measure your breasts
and if you show us skin
our mouths will salivate
while our minds hallucinate
about you.

You are the girl of our dreams
but you are a nightmare
to yourself.
For how will you ever be sure
Why he whispers in your ear, "I love you"?

Don't be angry at us.
He—we—cannot help
ourselves.

This lust for you
comes from within—
a seed planted by our
parents and their friends and enemies
who all got together
in harmony
to do this evil thing.

It is a reflex.
We do not deliberate
when we envision you
in our arms.
It is there (Now).

But you will enjoy your curse
for you never will be bored
you never will be alone
but Always, Always
you shall be lonely.
You can fool yourself sometimes,
and he can fool you too
because he is trained to do that
and you, too, are trained
and we are all trained
to fool each other
to fool ourselves
to live a lie.

And if anyone ever seeks the Truth
he will be mocked!
And if anyone ever finds the Truth
he will be isolated!
And if anyone ever tells the Truth
he will be killed!

so that everyone else can live a lie
in Peace.

Remember, pretty girl,
a sad search for Truth is better than
contentment with what is false.
There's no such thing as
Love without Truth
and, perhaps, if you seek Truth
you will find Love.

Particular Temptations for a Christian Girl

The Christian girl faces a host of temptations while playing the dating game. Indeed, the circumstances surrounding dating probably pose the greatest threat to the maintenance of her Christian commitment. I am not simply referring to the notion that some young people feel that they have to let down their sexual standards in order to gain popularity with the opposite sex. This may not be as true as a lot of people think it is.

1. Dates with non-Christians. More likely the greatest temptation will be to date those who aren't Christians and to develop deep relationships with them. Young people sometimes feel they are not worth much of anything unless they date. This kind of thinking leads to a willingness to settle for less than they should in areas of lasting importance. I know that it may seem narrow-minded to suggest that Christians should only date Christians. But nothing has greater potential for destroying a young girl's Christian commitment than a dating relationship with someone who doesn't share her faith.

The Apostle Paul says, "Do not be bound together with unbelievers" (2 Cor. 6:14). While the young girl may argue that she doesn't intend to marry the guy she's dating, her claim of "not being serious" is a bit naive. Dating is much more serious than most people think. The emotions during the dating period are intense, and dating arrangements often do lead to marriage. Many women have told me that they dated their husbands "just for fun," never intending to marry them because they weren't Christians. But they did end up together and the marriages have been less than completely happy.

2. *Playing dumb.* There is still another reason why dating tends to threaten the female's Christianity. In order to be good date bait, a female often has to pretend that she is less intelligent than she really is. Our world is filled with male chauvinists. Insecure males feel threatened by women who are very bright. Consequently, females often tend to play down their intelligence in order to entice males to like them. Few things upset me more than watching an intelligent woman conceal her brains for fear of losing out in the competition for dates.

In the college classroom, I find that females tend to do better in written tests and examinations than males. Yet, in spite of their obvious grasp of the material, these women very seldom participate in classroom discussions. They will sit there demurely, while males with half their knowledge take over the classroom debate. It bothers me to have to listen to asinine statements from some of my male students when I know that females who have much more to contribute will not speak out.

Traditionally, teenage females have refused to pursue the most prestigious professions for fear that their accomplishments might make them losers in the quest for marriage partners. Some choose to be nurses when they should be doctors. Others aim to be secretaries when they should be executives.

When females become less than they can be, they are failing the Lord. When God created us, He gave us definite potentialities. If we fail to become all that He created us to be, we are guilty of sin. It is interesting to note that in the Greek New Testament the word for sin is *hamartia,* which means, "to miss the mark." The New Testament suggests that *sin* is "failing to become all that you can be." This means that when a female fails to realize her highest potential because she is afraid to threaten the weak ego of an insecure male, she has compromised her faith.

Some will argue that I am overstating the case: they will contend that the dating game does not inflict anywhere near the amount of pain that I suggest. If you are among those who are skeptical about my assertions, let me remind you that just a couple of years ago the leading song on the hit parade was about the agonies of a dateless teenage girl. The lyrics of "At Seventeen" describe that suffering eloquently. A few phrases from the song express the pain of the girl who waits for what never comes to her: "ravaged faces," "inventing lovers," "dubious integrity," "ugly duckling girls," "cheat ourselves," and "ugly girls like me."

The song became popular because millions of teenage girls across America identified with its message. They bought over two million copies of the record because it articulated miseries that were too deep for them to express.

The Church and Dating

The church has failed to understand the desperate needs of young people who are buying into the success goals of society. Also, the church has paid very little attention to what is at stake in the dating game. Christians have felt content if they could keep the youth of the church sexually "pure" during the crucial teenage years. Young people have heard sermons and fireside chats on the necessity for sexual purity, but they seldom hear anything to help them work through the more complex problems related to dating. There is much that the church might do to help teenagers in these matters, and I would like to make a few suggestions.

The church should sponsor no activity that requires a partner of the opposite sex in order to participate. I have been intrigued by the fact that certain churches have banquets for their young people on the same night that the high school runs the senior prom. Their teenagers get all dressed up in formals and tuxedos, and gather in the church fellowship hall around the dinner tables to enjoy an evening of entertainment. While I see some value in such an activity, I wonder if some young people feel just as much left out of the church banquet as they would have from the school dance. These are the young people who, because they don't have dates, stay home while their peers go out for fun. It may be expected that the world will function in a way that makes certain people feel like rejects, but the church should never do this.

I have always liked walk-a-thons where young people look for sponsors to pay them a certain amount of money for each mile they walk for a worthy cause. The thing I like best about such group walks is that the basis for participation is not sexual attractiveness, but rather an altruistic concern for other people.

During walk-a-thons, young people often enjoy long talks with one another. Many times those who don't appear very special at the start become more attractive during the conversation and walk. Isn't it fascinating how the ways that people appear to us are altered as we get to know them in depth? Some friends that I now think are the most beautiful seemed plain to me when I first met them. And some people whom I thought to be stunning on first appearance proved less than attractive after a lengthy encounter.

Bike hikes, progressive dinners, and many other activities can be all-inclusive. Some young men in California have put together an organization known as Youth Specialties. They produce books giving churches hundreds of ideas to bring young people together. It is good to know that there are people within the church working in this area.

Above all else, it is necessary for Christians to communicate to young people the good news about Jesus. They must come to see that Jesus accepts them just as they are. They don't have to make any team or do some great deed or be beautiful. They are loved infinitely and appreciated intensely for what they are. Young people desperately need the message that acceptance by Jesus is not something which needs to be earned.

7
Symptoms
of
Mid-life Males

The North American male wins success primarily through his vocation. His status, income, and ability to exercise power over others are all wrapped up with his occupation. It is even safe to say that vocation is usually the means whereby male identity is achieved.

When a man meets a stranger, usually the first question asked of him is, "What do you do for a living?" People evaluate him and define his social significance when they learn his vocation. Since an individual's self-concept is largely based on what he feels significant others think of him, such a definition of social significance has great importance.

Because the male's social identity is so tied to his vocation, it is important for us to be reminded that there can be a difference between what a person *is* and what he *does*. What a person *is* is usually so much deeper and more significant than what he *does* that knowing his vocation may give only a hint of his true identity.

Christians should know better than to evaluate the significance of a person totally in terms of his vocation. We are supposed to be people who do not live according to our sinful nature but according to the Spirit (Rom. 8:4). This means that we do not use the same criteria as society does to evaluate individuals. Unfortunately, Christians do not always live in accord with the Scripture's admonition. In an overwhelming number of churches, the tendency is to evaluate people in much the same way as the secular world evaluates them.

Imagine a Sunday morning at a typical American church. A new couple comes in and finds a place to sit in one of the pews. In a small church, most of the congregation will wonder who they are, and the pastor will pay special attention to them as he sits with his posed reverence on the pulpit chair. As soon as the service is over, some church members will make sure that the new couple feels welcome. Some of the key members will immediately surround them and ask, "What's your name?" The second question, probably aimed at the man, will be, "What do you do?"

If he tells them that he is the newly hired teacher at the junior high school, you can imagine the response. Someone will wave over the Sunday School superintendent and whisper, "He's the new junior high school teacher in town." The superintendent is likely to shoot a quick prayer up to the Lord, "Thank Thee, Jesus. That junior high class hast wiped out four teachers in a row and lo, Thou hast provided still another." The elated conversation will probably end with someone saying, "If you haven't found a church home, we certainly hope that you make this your church. We could really *use* you."

The man's vocation has been the basis for evaluation and he has been approved because he can be *used* in the work of the church. No one knows if he loves Christ or is commited to Christian service or if he has a grasp of the Scriptures.

Erich Fromm once said that the problem with our age is that we love things and use people instead of using things and loving people. Maybe the church could take a page from the writings of this great humanist. We should be considering people in terms of how we can love them, not in terms of how we might use them.

Too often the church uses people for ministries to which God has never called them.

Prestige vs. Person

It is interesting to note that Jesus did not choose His disciples from among those who held prestigious positions in society. Instead, He chose a couple of fishermen, a tax collector (they were bad people in those days), and two troublemakers who were called the "Sons of Thunder." Some of the women who followed Jesus were unimpressive and one had a reputation so low that people murmured against the Lord for associating with her.

Christ looked within people and tried to discern their hungers, dreams, and values, and ultimately their faith. In our hurried age, we haven't the time to gain an in-depth analysis of persons. We meet people casually and want some quick and simple way to judge them. And too often we evaluate them according to vocation.

Sociologists have studied our system of stratifying people and have compiled a list of vocations in accord with the prestige that we assign to them. Starting from the top, we give priority to occupations in the following order: professional and technical workers; farmers and farm managers; managers and administrators, except farm; clerical workers; sales workers; craftsmen, foremen; operatives; private household workers; service workers, except private household; farm laborers, nonfarm laborers.

Those who have vocations near the top of this list are often very impressed with their own success, and desire to impress others with their roles in society. To make sure that strangers quickly find out what they do, some people in these professions try to manipulate conversations so that they can talk about their prominence.

Once I was at a party with a friend who is a medical doctor. Since I was the only one he knew at the gathering, he stayed close to me. It was interesting to watch and listen as he entered into conversations with various people throughout the evening. For some reason they were failing to ask him what he did for a living and that upset him. I watched him become increasingly anxious as he tried to work into the conversations hints about his profession, hoping that when people realized he was a doctor they would respect him. He became so deliberate that by the end of the evening I felt that he was about to stand on a chair and yell, "Look at me! I'm a doctor! Why aren't you impressed?"

While no one is denying the importance of vocation, as Christians we know that many people who have prestigious vocations are hollow and superficial. On the other hand, many individuals whose vocational status is not highly ranked by society prove to possess spiritual qualities which make them great people to know.

When my boy was in third grade, he came home and explained that his homework assignment that day was to prepare a talk on the topic, "What I want to be when I grow up."

I told him, "Tell your teacher that when you grow up you want to be a fully realized human being like Jesus. Tell her that what she meant to ask was what you want to *do* to earn money." He told her, and it didn't go over well at all.

It is important to impress on children that in the Christian value system, being a successful person is far more important than having a prestigious vocation. Christians should realize that it is possible for people to have a deep sense of success, even when the world is unimpressed by them. And vice versa, it is possible for people to awe society with their accomplishments but inwardly to feel like failures.

Prestige for the Family

Married men know that their vocations determine not only their own positions in society, but also provide status for their wives and children. They know that their children will gain prestige among their friends if they can brag about what their fathers do. So much is the social standing of children connected with the successes of their fathers that children will often argue among themselves as to whose father has the most important job.

Women are also conscious of the fact that their status is tied to their husbands' vocations. When they marry, many women give careful consideration to the vocation of potential mates, for they know that their places in society will be determined by the social positions of their husbands.

We all know women who have driven their husbands to become successful because that success would reflect on them. Shakespeare's Lady Macbeth was not the only woman in history guilty of self-interest as she expressed ambition for her husband.

One of the cries of the modern feminists is that women should be free to determine their places in society through their own achievements. If the feminists succeed, some men might experience welcome relief from the pressures of wives ambitious for vicarious success.

Mid-life Crisis

A society in which vocational achievement is the most important indicator of success is an ideal environment for a condition known as the "mid-life crisis." This usually hits a man sometime after he passes the age of 40. The rapid succession of promotions of earlier years has slowed down and he feels that he is not going anywhere. As he watches the younger people in his profession who seem to be moving ahead of him, he knows that he is no longer viewed as the promising executive. Rather, he has become an established bureaucrat, nervously protecting his job against the assaults of the "young Turks." In these middle years, the self-confidence that formerly verged on arrogance is dramatically shaken.

Middle-aged men who feel that they are not sufficiently appreciated by their companies often develop resentments toward people who gain the positions that they themselves desired. Feeling threatened and hurt, they often react with pettiness, attaching great importance to every symbol of prestige. The size of another man's desk, the kind of office equipment, the location of the office, the amount of secretarial help—all can take on exaggerated importance. It is not so much a need for these things as that these symbols provide desperately needed assurances of personal importance. It is pathetic to see a once proud man bickering over such trifles.

Sometimes these threatened males have their greatest fears realized, as jobs are phased out. When men in their middle years suddenly find that their services are no longer required, their egos are shattered and their self-confidence is gone. Often their personal wealth is diminished and like Willie Loman in Arthur Miller's play, *Death of a Salesman*, they see little left to live for.

It is hard for a throwaway executive or unemployed factory worker not to feel contempt for himself. He sold himself to the demands of the job, tailoring his personality to the expectations of his role. He compromised his personal integrity in order to fit the expectations of "the organization man." He said the right things, held the proper political views, attended the right church, and joined the right country club in his effort to establish the proper image. Having become what he thought his company wanted, he now feels betrayed.

Soren Kierkegaard once said, "When a man aspires to be a Caesar and fails to become a Caesar, he will hate what he is because he is not Caesar." He meant that the man who fails to achieve what he sets out to achieve will end up hating himself.

Fortunately, most men do not lose their jobs during the mid-life crisis. But even those who remain employed often find their jobs increasingly meaningless and come home emotionally dissipated at the end of the day. Paul Goodman, a prominent social critic of the 1960s, pointed out that there has never been a time in world history when men have worked less hard and come home more tired. That tiredness is not from physical exertion but from the emotional emptiness of not doing anything that seems worthwhile.

Escape Routes at Mid-life

Men choose from a variety of escape routes, trying to bypass the depressions of mid-life.

1. Sports. It is frightening to see a middle-aged man devoting large segments of his life to vicariously experiencing the thrill of stardom with his favorite ball players. He has little time for conversation, in-depth relationships, or the simple joys of family life because his life is consumed with being a television spectator. "The thrill of victory and the agony of defeat" are larger in his consciousness than the thrills and agonies of his own experience or that of his family. His own existence becomes less real to him than his favorite ball players. He knows more about the personal lives of athletes than he does about what is going on in the lives of his own children. His emotional state is often determined by whether his favorite teams win or lose. Sometimes such a man will become so depressed when his favorite team loses that he commits suicide.

Evangelical Christians who frown on "the pleasures of the world" often fail to see the destructive potential in the American preoccupation with sports. While sports may provide wholesome fun for Christians, in more situations than we would like to admit, sports can also eat up precious time, leaving people with little room in their lives for personal relationships or Christian service.

We must recognize that intense devotion to sports can become idolatrous, taking the place of God. This is certainly the case for the man who finds sports to be an escape from the meaninglessness of his everyday existence.

2. Consumerism. Another false escape route from the mid-life crisis is found in "buying things." We live in a consumer-oriented society. The ads on television attempt to convince us that we can gain a sense of meaning and fulfillment by purchasing the right things. There used to be a beer ad that played on our awareness of life slipping away: "You only go through life once, so why not reach for gusto?" Of course, the ad promised that gusto could be gained by purchasing a six-pack of beer. Reflecting personal insecurities, another beer ad tells us, "You tell the world you know what you're doing. . . ."

Soft drinks are sold on the basis that they will make us young.

The ads for men's clothing claim that success is tied to wearing the right styles and colors.

It did not take Vance Packard to convince us that automobiles have provided Americans with far more than a means of transportation. They have become symbolic statements of who we are. An individual is saying something to the world when he drives a Mercedes Benz.

Our country's love affair with the big automobile is tied to the desire of many Americans for significance. This has been particularly true in the minority community. Show me the man who has been diminished by our social system and I'll show you a man with a strong tendency to assert that he is somebody, by sitting behind the wheel of a flashy car.

Within the context of such a consumer-oriented society, it is no surprise that many people meet the mid-life crisis by buying more and more things. They hope to silence the gnawing awareness that they have failed to become what they hoped to be.

This escape route often has disastrous effects, as people extend their credit and mortgage their futures. Even Christians, who should know better, have bought piles of things they really didn't need, in an attempt to drive out their feelings of emptiness and failure.

The American society has facilitated this tendency to self-destruction by providing credit cards and easy loans to people whose buying habits have become a sickness. The church must prophetically declare that the American media are wrong. In spite of what the ads declare, people cannot buy their way out of a sense of worthlessness. A great sadness comes when a person senses that failure in his vocation cannot be driven away by purchasing things. A voice still echos down the corridors of time, saying, "Why do you spend . . . your wages for what does not satisfy?" (Isa. 55:2)

3. *Work.* Some American males deal with their mid-life uncertainties by becoming workaholics. If they work 12 to 18 hours a day, they never have to reflect upon their emotional state.

Blaise Pascal once said, "All evil stems from this—that men do not know how to handle solitude." What Pascal was trying to tell us is that in solitude, men are forced to reflect upon the meaning of their own lives. In solitude they are forced to come to grips with who they are and what they have become. Many men fill their lives with work so that they do not have to confront such solitude.

Most workaholics tend to make their jobs too important, attaching fantastic significance to every little thing they do. If their work is of great importance, then they must be important. They often become so bogged down in the imagined significance of trivia that their jobs become too much for them. For this reason, workaholism is usually self-defeating.

What the workaholic fears most is not death, but times of reflection in which he sees what he has become. Kierkegaard says we are like smooth pebbles thrown over the surface of a lake. We dance along the surface until we run out of momentum and then sink to a hundred thousand fathoms of nothingness. The workaholic knows that he cannot go on working forever. Sooner or later, he must stop; work is only a temporary escape from nothingness.

4. Children. Many children find themselves pushed to achievement by fathers who try to live through the successes of their offspring, and so escape their own failures.

My boy is a member of his high school basketball team. The father of a player on his team came to every practice to watch his son go through the workouts and drills. The other boys became aware that this father was trying to live through his boy. My son joked about the man until one day he realized that the boy himself was painfully aware of what his father was doing.

5. Affairs. One of the most disastrous escape routes from the mid-life crisis is the extramarital affair. Such an affair is particularly alluring if the partner is a younger woman, because the man is temporarily assured that he is not over the hill, but is still young enough to believe in his future. His own wife knows him too well and urges him toward the reality of what he has become. Since the new younger woman doesn't know him well, she can help him play a game of make-believe. She serves a useful purpose as she becomes his significant other, reflecting to him an image of the mature power figure he always wanted to be. Even though she perpetrates a myth, he loves it.

It is important to note that it is the way she makes him *feel* that attracts him. He doesn't really love her—he is too empty to love anyone. When she no longer serves his purpose, he will drop her and look for somebody else to give him emotional support. Few are so vulnerable to extramarital affairs as men who are experiencing the mid-life crisis. Even as far back as the Kinsey study, the evidence was clear that among middle-class men, the tendency toward extramarital affairs was most pronounced in their early 40s.

Christian men often have sufficient grounding in the teachings of Scripture so as not to become sexually involved outside of marriage. However, many such men who would never "touch" a woman can become emotionally involved with extramarital partners in ways that can prove to be dehumanizing to their wives, and deceptive to themselves. Time and time again, I have counseled men who have not been sexually unfaithful, but who have allowed women other than their wives to become their significant others. This is a very common practice among clergymen, who often find in their congregations attractive younger women who are escaping from their own empty lives through romantic fantasies. Such arrangements are often clothed in phony nobility, as the partners blasphemously suggest that it is their loyalty to Christ that keeps them from going to bed together. In their pretense of Christlike behavior, they massage each others' egos, at the expense of their respective mates.

One time a woman sat crying in my office as she told me that her husband was having an affair. I asked her if she had any evidence of this—did she find a note, lipstick on the collar, or a motel slip? She quickly responded by saying, "Oh, I think I could survive the knowledge that my husband was keeping a whore on the side as long as I knew that I was his companion and partner; but it's the other way around. That other woman is his companion and partner and I am his whore!''

The husband in this story was a prominent Christian leader who had dehumanized his wife by making her into a sex partner, while denying her the intimacy of companionship and partnership in life. In a legalistic sense he had not committed adultery, but one wonders how many times while having sex with his wife, he had imagined himself with the other woman.

It is amazing how cruel Christians can be while pretending to uphold the letter of God's Law. No wonder Jesus pointed out that even if a man does not sleep with a woman, he still may be committing adultery with her in his fantasies.

This escape route leads nowhere. It is only a matter of time before the new arrangement loses its value as an escape from meaninglessness. Then the man will have to move on to another affair, as he seeks to buttress his faltering ego. Like Don Juan, he has failed to see that the absence of lasting gratification is not in his sexual partner but in his own inadequacy.

8
Hope
for the
43-year-old Man

The first step toward overcoming the mid-life crisis is for a man to keep himself in good health, and well-rested. Middle-aged men need to realize that they can no longer physically exert themselves as they did when they were 25 years old, that they tire more quickly and need their rest. It is amazing how much more easily I can manage my life when I have eaten properly and had enough sleep. Men in their 40s need vacation time to psychologically recuperate from the stress of their everyday lives. Unfortunately, not everyone can go to the Bahamas to get himself together again. But for those who can afford it, such a trip is worth the money, and could be less expensive than paying a psychiatrist. The mind and the body are intricately related and when the body is worn out, the mind is affected.

Change of Perspective

The mid-life crisis should encourage a man to reexamine his life, to clarify his values, and to look at what he has achieved. It's a time to determine priorities and decide what should be of ultimate significance in life. Sometimes men find that when they consider what is *really* important and what is *relatively* important, they have nothing about which to be depressed and much for which to give thanks.

A sense of failure may result from a man's perspective on life. If he changes that perspective, he may feel like a different man. It is even possible for him to look at his vocation in a new way and to find real significance in his work.

Christopher Wren, the architect who designed so many of the great churches of London, told of walking through the building site of St. Paul's Cathedral, asking the various workers what they were doing. One explained that he was doing carpentry work, another that he was laying bricks, still another that he was putting stained-glass windows into place, and a fourth claimed to be carving stone. As he left the cathedral, Wren came upon a man mixing mortar and asked him what he was doing. The mason, not recognizing the architect, proudly responded, "Sir, I am building a great cathedral."

However others might have described this man's work was of little consequence. By the grace of God, he was able to see his labor as a service to the Lord and to humanity. For him, the mundane took on a sacred quality, giving his task new significance.

Change of Occupation

Unfortunately, for most men this change of perspective doesn't help. In spite of efforts to find meaning, they come away from their labor with a sense of having wasted their lives. To such men, I can say, "Why not consider a change?"

The middle years might prove to be a good time to change your vocation, and go into something that offers a new challenge. I have seen men whose lives were routinized into boredom, who had lost their sense of aliveness, be emotionally reborn by changing vocations and doing something that they had always dreamed of doing.

I know some men in their early 40s who have gone back to

college and seminary in order to prepare for the ministry. I teach part-time at a seminary, and find that my best students are the middle-aged men who, during a mid-life crisis, decided to become servants of the church. The dean of our seminary feels that these are the men who make the best pastors. They go into churches knowing the complexities that so many members of the congregation face, and which younger pastors cannot possibly comprehend.

George Foreman, the onetime heavyweight boxing champion, picked himself up from a defeat at the hands of Muhammed Ali and gave himself over to Christian service. He admits that he misses boxing, but contends he has found such joy in preaching the Gospel that he would never go back to the ring. He points out that he enjoys telling people about the love of God and that it would be hard for him to express that love to a man whom he was beating up in a boxing ring.

A recent example of a radical mid-life change is Chuck Colson. Many people refuse to accept what has happened to this Watergate conspirator. In his 40s, crushed by his own mistakes, he discovered that he could find meaning in a life of Christian service. He has developed an organization which provides special ministries to men and women who are in prison. Colson has created a life of significance out of personal disaster.

Albert Schweitzer at the age of 40 had achieved fame as one of the great interpreters of Bach, had written a book that became a theological classic among seminary students throughout the world, and was a wealthy man. Schweitzer was successful in the eyes of the world, but he did not feel fulfilled. At the age of 40 he left it all for the interior of equatorial Africa to serve as a missionary. One doesn't have to agree with the theology of Albert Schweitzer to admire his commitment to service.

If you have approached your work in a Christlike spirit, endeavoring to find meaning in your labor, but are receiving no satisfaction from what you are doing, I would advise you to change vocations. I don't know where God wants you to be, but I know that God *does not* want you to be in a job that denies you fulfillment or diminishes your humanity. God created you in His image and, like your Lord, you are to creatively delight in your work.

When I was a boy, my father worked for the Radio Corporation of America as a cabinetmaker. He fashioned and polished those wooden consoles that housed the complex array of tubes and wires necessary to have good radio reception in the early days of the wireless. He was a craftsman, and though he did not get paid much for his labor, he felt a tremendous sense of gratification from what he produced. Every time he made a radio console, he put his initials on the back of it. I remember when we visited friends or relatives he would motion for me to look in the back of the console to see if his initials were there. Whenever I found them, he would nearly burst with pride. That wooden console was more than just a thing. In some mystical way he had extended himself into the production of his own product. Each console was *his*, an expression of his skills and abilities. Because he had pride in his work, he was a fulfilled man.

Today, not many workers have the privilege of finding that type of fulfillment in their labors. Paul Goodman points out that over 80 percent of those employed in the American work force hate what they do. Thank God that wasn't true of my father.

Most of us must turn to little children to see people engrossed in their work. Have you ever watched the boys and girls working on crafts during a session of Vacation Bible School? The child who wants to make something for his mother works with a dedication and intensity that has become all too rare in our age of shoddy workmanship. I can still see my little boy coming home from school and handing me a piece of clay that was painted green and saying, "I made it for you." Every worker should strive for that kind of emotional payoff from his labors.

Some years ago, a friend of mine went to teach English literature at a state college. He was there for three weeks when he went into the dean's office to say that he was quitting.

"I'm not coming back next week and I thought you ought to know," he said. The dean replied, "If you walk out on your contract, you're not going to teach here again. What's more, you won't teach anywhere, if I can help it."

After my friend left his job, his mother contacted me by phone and said I had to see him. She was sure he had gone crazy and hoped I could talk him into going back to his job.

I found my friend Charlie living in an attic apartment in Hamilton Square, New Jersey. I must admit that his apartment had style: travel posters pasted all over the walls, a good assortment of books scattered around the room, and the stereo playing a Wagnerian opera. I sat down in a beanbag chair that swallowed me up. After we had exchanged niceties, I came to the point.

"What have you done?" I asked.

"I quit," said Charlie. "I walked out. I don't want to teach anymore. Every time I walked into that classroom, I died a little bit."

I could understand him. I am a teacher, and I know what it is like to go into class and pour out your heart to students, to let every nerve inside you tingle with the excitement of your most profound insights. I know what it is like to passionately share the struggles of your existence, to lay your soul bare in an attempt to communicate your deepest feelings. Then, when it is all over, some student in the back of the room raises his hand and says, "Do we have to know this stuff for the final?"—and I die a little bit too.

It wasn't long before I realized that Charlie was not about to go back into the classroom; so I asked him what he was doing with himself these days. He said, "I'm a mailman."

Reaching back into the value system provided by the Protestant work ethic, I said to him, "Charlie, if you're going to be a mailman, be the best mailman in the world!"

He said, "I am a *lousy* mailman. Everybody else who delivers mail gets back to the post office by about two o'clock. I never get back until six."

"What takes you so long?" I asked.

"I visit," said Charlie. "You'd never believe how many lonely people there were on my route who had never been visited until I became a mailman. What's more, now I can't sleep at night."

"Why can't you sleep?" I asked.

"Have you ever tried to sleep after drinking 15 cups of coffee?" was his reply.

As I sat and looked at my friend Charlie, I envied him. He was alive with the excitement that comes to a person doing something meaningful with his life. Because he moved from being a college professor to being a mailman, he has lost status. But what difference does that make? As Charlie invests himself significantly in the lives of other people, he is finding fulfillment in visiting "orphans and widows in their distress" (James 1:27).

People in their early 40s find it difficult to change jobs. As meaningless as many jobs are, they do offer a sense of security. W.I. Thomas, one of the founders of American sociology, analyzing the basic wishes of human existence, notes that all people have a desire for security and a desire for new adventure. Thomas sees these two wishes in diametrical opposition to each other. The older we get, the more our desire for security grows and our desire for new adventure diminishes. But this does not have to be. One of the results of the new life in Christ is that "your old men dream dreams, your young men will see visions" (Joel 2:28).

I am always thrilled by the story of that old man Abraham, who, when he was 75, decided to start life anew. The Bible says that when Abraham was called by God, he left the Ur of the Chaldees, "not knowing where he was going" (Heb. 11:8). He saw that there was more to his life that was waiting to be lived. If Abraham dared to strike out in a new direction at the age of 75, why should a man of 40 be afraid to do so?

A commitment to Christ can enable us to be adventuresome because our need for security is gratified, not in our vocations, but in our trust in Jesus. When we commit our lives to Christ, we sense that He will be with us and support us and uphold us throughout all of life. With security we can say, "If God is for us, who is against us?" (Rom. 8:31)

Invest in Family

In the attempt to create meaning out of the sense of absurdity that marks the mid-life crisis, a man should take a good look at his family. In his rush to be a success, he may have overlooked the precious opportunity of having deep relationships with his wife and children. Fortunately, a man in his early 40s still has time to develop the kind of family relationships that will give him a sense of success, even when all else might be making him feel that life is a failure. Too often, we become so preoccupied with our occupational roles that we let opportunities for intimacy slip away from us. Then, like Tevye in *Fiddler on the Roof* we ask, "Where is the little girl I carried? Where is the little boy at play? I don't remember growing older—when, oh when did they?"

Often, the mid-life crisis causes men to pay intense attention to those precious ones they had previously ignored. Such men discover the joy that comes from listening to their children, helping them with their problems, and wonderfully sharing their joys. These men discover, before it is too late, that there is a fantastic fulfillment in looking into their children's eyes when they speak, discerning not only what is being said but what is being felt and meant.

In Thornton Wilder's play, *Our Town*, a woman who has died is allowed to relive one day of her life. She chooses her 12th birthday. Other dead people try to warn her not to do it, but she insists. As she watches herself and her family members live out that day, she is overwhelmed with despair at the way members of her family just take each other for granted. She agonizes over the fact that they talk to each other without really paying attention, and she ends up crying, "Don't they realize that they won't have each other forever?"

If a mid-life crisis shakes men out of ignoring those who are most precious to them, and causes them to give themselves to their families in an intense manner, it can then lead a man to a more meaningful life than he has ever known before.

Create Community

Another option for men facing the mid-life crisis is found in the creating of community. The American family system has tended to isolate the members of the nuclear family from an extended network of blood relatives. Most people lack meaningful emotional ties with persons outside of their immediate families. In times of crisis the family is left alone, lacking a support group that could carry them through such difficult times.

In the face of this separateness, some Christian families have made decisions to establish community with other families. Sometimes, such Christian families choose to live next door to each other, so that they can share with one another in many ways. As men and women develop deep friendships, they learn that the American tendency to glorify individuality at the expense of community is wrong. Jesus has created us to be members one of another, and in community we find the emotional support that can carry us through crises that might otherwise threaten our identities and concepts of self-worth.

I am suggesting that couples make a covenant with one or more other couples to remain together throughout life. I use the word *covenant* because it connotes a sacred, binding relationship. If there is a commitment to be mutually supportive, one couple will not move away from the others, even to take advantage of job opportunities that would move them up the success ladder. In order to maintain community, they are willing to stay with their friends, no matter what the vocational price, because the emotional payoff makes it worthwhile.

When several families live close by each other, it becomes possible to adopt a more inexpensive lifestyle. Instead of buying several lawnmowers, the families can buy one and share it. The same can be done with ladders, electric saws, and washing machines. Food is purchased in quantity and hence, at reduced costs. In sort, it is possible to cut the cost of living in middle-class American comfort.

Surrender to Christ

In the midst of the mid-life crisis, men need Jesus. A total surrender to Christ enables men to learn how to overcome the bitterness and resentment that they have harbored toward those who seem to be beating them out in the race for vocational success. They find that Christ gives them a graciousness that enables them to love their competitors and to forgive those who are ready to do them dirt in the competition to get ahead.

When Jesus becomes the Significant Other in men's lives, they sense how ultimately important they are. As they recognize that Jesus loves them and accepts them as they are, it becomes easier for them to love and accept themselves. In Christ, men learn that the praise of the world has no lasting significance. They learn the truth of a verse that before seemed like a cliche, "Only one life, 'twill soon be past; only what's done for Christ will last." They see that it is never too late to do those things that store up "treasures in heaven, where neither moth nor rust destroys, and where thieves do not break in or steal" (Matt. 6:20).

What Is Success?

Jesus puts emphasis on little things we do in love rather than the big things that impress other people. Our Lord described Judgment Day as a time in which some will say, "Lord, we cast out demons, we healed people, we did many works in Your name." And Jesus will respond to those who thought that they had done great things in the eyes of the world by saying, "Get away from Me, you workers of iniquity. I never knew you." (See Matthew 7:22–23.)

On Judgment Day, the Lord will reveal the value of actions that seemed relatively unimportant. He will give special recognition to those who fed the hungry, clothed the naked, visited the sick and the imprisoned, and will declare that those who have done such things are the most blessed in the kingdom of God. "Inasmuch as ye have done it unto the least of these, My brethren, ye have done it unto Me." (See Matthew 25:35–40.)

Many men have found success in taking advantage of opportunities to express love in simple ways. It is more important to express love in the little things that we can do for one another day by day than to gain fame in the eyes of the world. Christians believe that if they are faithful in these small things, the Lord will make them rulers over great things. They know that those who seek to be first become last, but those who are willing to be last and servants of all will be elevated to positions of prominence in the kingdom of God.

9
Pressures
on the
Mid-life Woman

It used to be fairly simple to figure out what a woman had to do to be successful. She had to marry a decent, hardworking, successful man. The "better" she married, the more successful she would be. Her teenage years were aimed at developing those traits which would make her a desirable marital partner, because men in the rural society of bygone generations demanded far more than physical attractiveness and a pleasant personality in a potential mate. Not that good looks and a congenial manner were unimportant, but a young, aspiring farmer was also looking for someone who could cook, sew, keep house, milk cows, help in the planting, and perform a host of other chores that were part of a well-run farm. A young man was told that beauty was only skin deep; if he was awed by the physical attractiveness of some woman, those who cared about his future would ask, "Can she bake a cherry pie, Billy Boy, Billy Boy?"

When America moved into the urban, industrial lifestyle, it left many of those old role requirements behind. It is no longer necessary for a woman to spend many hours every day preparing food for her household, because food is industrially processed and packaged. With relative ease, the modern woman can open a can of this, a package of that, and have an edible dinner on the table in almost no time at all. While some women delight in sewing, the majority of the clothing worn by Americans is industrially manufactured. Since most men are not farmers, they do not need wives who can plow fields and milk cows.

The role of a woman has changed because her social situation has changed. She can no longer gain a sense of personal worth by performing those essential tasks which belonged to her in the agrarian society. Increasingly, her self-image has become dependent on her husband's opinion of her. Now, more than ever, he is the significant other who provides her with whatever sense of success she possesses. If he thinks she is a wonderful person, then she will view herself that way. But if he regards her as an unattractive, uninteresting, and worthless person, in all probability, she will end up feeling like a failure.

The woman in today's world is constantly told that she has "never had it so good." Yet, in many ways her life has never been more difficult. Instead of the neatly defined roles prescribed for her in the past, the modern female is thrust into a complicated multiplicity of roles. She comes and goes in an endless round of exhausting activity, and is frequently left without any sense of fulfillment.

The middle-class wife in today's society is expected to be a good hostess, a community volunteer, an interior decorator, a gourmet cook, a good conversationalist, an efficient purchasing agent, and a sex partner who has overcome prudish restraints.

As a mother, she is to be a social director for the clubs her children join, and a taxi driver who can take the children to and from their endless array of lessons, sports, and clubs. She is supposed to be a teacher's aide who can help the children with their homework assignments, type their papers, help them with projects, and maintain communications with the teachers at school. She is expected to do all of these things while still keeping the house clean, washing the clothes, cooking the meals and coordinating the life of the family.

It is no wonder that today's woman often feels depressed over not being able to get everything done. Her family members often take what she does for granted, giving little consideration to the time and effort expended. What is worse is that often she herself does not recognize the amount of time and energy that these taken-for-granted activities require. At the end of a day, she often feels exhausted and perplexed as she wonders, "Where did my day go and why wasn't I able to get more done?"

Poor Preparation for Motherhood

The modern woman has had little preparation for her tiring and demanding roles. She was educated in schools that gave her the same training as her husband. In college, she learned to enjoy the poetry of T.S. Eliot, the paintings of Monet, and a philosophical approach to the humanities. When she married and had children, this life was suddenly interrupted when she was thrust into an endless round of chores alien to her background. She found herself mixing baby formula, changing diapers, curing rashes, and maintaining endless surveillance over the activities and bodily functions of her children.

Whatever positive things one can say about being a mother, it must be readily admitted that the middle-class female finds that becoming one does interrupt her former lifestyle. Often, the change is an abrupt cultural shock, and proves difficult to manage.

George Herbert Mead, considered by many to be America's greatest social philosopher, claimed that the games played in childhood prepare us for roles we later assume in life. He contended that children act out in play the kinds of roles that they will assume in adulthood. By this play, they become psychologically prepared for their future tasks, and to some degree, conditioned for what they will later experience.

Today's young woman lacked the kind of play activity that

would have psychologically prepared her for her role. In all probability she did not play with a doll that wet its pants, cried "Mama," and was carted around in a toy carriage. The contemporary mother probably played with a Barbie doll as a child. Barbie is a grown-up doll, a career girl in her early 20s. She has gowns and tennis outfits; she drives a convertible, and has a kid sister and a boyfriend named Ken. When the childhood play habits of the modern woman cause her to identify with the footloose and fancy-free lifestyle of a career woman, she is denied some of the preparation that would make adjustment to motherhood a lot easier.

Raising Children Alone

It must be noted that no woman in history has been left so alone to face the responsibilities of childrearing as has the contemporary mother. In earlier times, people lived in small communities, surrounded by kinfolk or intimate friends. These close associates often had a wealth of experience in motherhood that they shared with the new mother. They also took care of the child from time to time, providing her with needed rest and relief. If she wanted to go to town with her husband, there was always an aunt, an in-law, a sister, or a close neighbor who would come in and mind the children. If a mother wasn't feeling well, there was usually some competent adult who would care for the child, while the mother got some rest. It is only today's mother, isolated in the modern urban world, who has had to resort to that strange curiosity called a "baby-sitter."

In today's world, the woman who is part of a small, mobile family unit may find herself isolated in some high-rise apartment, surrounded by strangers. When she is sick there is no one to call for help. As her husband leaves in the morning, the best that he can offer her is the promise of a telephone call during the day to see how she's doing.

Compare what the modern woman endures when raising a child to the experiences of mothers in ancient times. Specifically, compare the modern woman with Mary, the mother of Jesus. When her Boy was 12 years of age, she took Him to the temple in Jerusalem for His Bar Mitzvah. When Mary and Joseph headed home, Jesus decided to stay behind and talk with the scribes and the scholars. He had many questions that needed answering. It wasn't until a whole day's journey had transpired that Mary and Joseph realized that Jesus was not with them. Can't you just imagine Joseph saying to Mary, "I haven't seen Jesus since early morning."

The Scriptures tell us that Mary and Joseph "supposed that He had been with the others." Mary and Joseph were part of a supportive community that lovingly cared for all of its children. In the ancient world, a young mother did not raise a child by herself, but was aided in that task by a group of people who brought responsibility, experience, and knowledge to the childrearing process. It is a peculiarity of our time that a woman is left to raise children on her own.

Because so much is demanded of the modern woman, for which she is so poorly prepared, it is difficult for her to feel successful. Often she cannot handle the demands of her life, and she may become angry or depressed when everybody seems to suggest that she has it so easy.

Life in a Sexist Society

On top of all of this, the modern woman is subjected to the psychological consequences of living in a sexist society. When we call a society *sexist,* we are describing a social system in which females must maintain certain physical attributes and a certain personality style in order to be deemed worthwhile. In such a society, a competent female may be treated like a loser if she doesn't have a pretty face, a proper body shape, and prescribed mannerisms. Lacking these attributes, she may suffer from deep feelings of inferiority, regardless of how bright or efficient she is.

What is worse, she is expected to maintain these desirable physical traits throughout most of her life, even though it is impossible to do so. When she begins to lose her youthful looks, she may feel threatened, particularly if her husband takes an interest in younger women who seem to possess what she has lost. In her middle-aged years, she is supposed to smile benevolently as her husband drools over younger women who parade before him on the beach, clad in bathing suits that conceal far less than they reveal. She doesn't like to admit it, but she is hurt when her husband finds their physical appearance more attractive than hers. In many ways he subtly communicates that she no longer turns him on.

It is no wonder that the suicide rate for married women over the age of 35 is three times higher than it is for men of the same age, and that the number of women in middle-age suffering from emotional depression far exceeds the number of men experiencing the same malady. Kate Millet explains it well when she says that men at the age of 40 can be considered mature, while women at the age of 40 are usually considered obsolete. This is not to suggest that there aren't attractive 40-year-old women, but only to point out that women who are attractive at that age are considered so because they don't look 40.

I have spoken at Christian Women's Club meetings all across this nation. In almost every case, the woman chairing the meeting has told me, "There are three things that we do not talk about at the Christian Women's Club meetings: church affiliation, weight, and age." They know all too well that when women are made conscious of their age and weight, they are simultaneously made conscious that those charms of the "successful woman" are slipping away from them. There is no question but that society, by overemphasizing the importance of physical attractiveness in women, helps to make them feel like failures when their looks are eroded by the passage of time.

Feminist Arguments

Politically conservative members of the evangelical community usually fail to see the legitimacy of many of the feminist arguments. Conservatives are too easily sidetracked from these concerns by political arguments over the pros and cons of the Equal Rights Amendment. It is important for Christians to understand that, whatever their views may be on the constitutional changes sought by the feminist movement, these angry women also represent a righteous indignation against what the modern world does to women. It overtaxes them with impossible role expectations and dehumanizes them by attaching so much of their personal worth to their physical appearance. While Jesus would have rejected some of the claims of the women's liberation leaders, He would have hailed their efforts to end so many of the unnecessary hurts which society inflicts upon modern women.

A careful examination of the social rebellion fostered by the feminist movement brings us to an awareness of the positions that should be supported by Christians.

1. Beauty contests. In the earliest stages of the feminist movement, some members demonstrated in Atlantic City against the Miss America contest. The feminists saw the contest as something that oppressed women and diminished their sense of worth. Indeed it has surprised me that more evangelicals have not joined them in this crusade. Surely those of us who are opposed to pornography should sense that there is something wrong about a contest that has more than 50 women parading their sexual wares before the lustful eyes of millions of American men. I don't want to sound like a prude, but I think the feminists are right when they say that such contests treat women as if they were pieces of meat, instead of persons.

I know that many of the Miss America contestants teach Sunday School and are ''Christian girls.'' I know that several of them have given testimonies as to what Christ means to them. But none of that detracts from the fact that the Miss America contest is wrong. One young woman who had been a participant in the contest heard one of my tirades against it and complained to me that the Miss America contest is more than just a display of flesh in bathing suits.

I agree, but because it *does* require a display of flesh in bathing suits as part of its selection process, I believe it must be condemned.

It is amazing to me that Christians are not more irate over what goes on at Atlantic City in the early part of September. Consider that each of the contestants has the various parts of her body measured and then broadcast to the world. As the emcee tells us that Miss America is 36-26-36, women all across America quietly compare their own measurements to this prescribed shape, and most of them come away feeling significantly inferior.

It is interesting to note that for years the Roman Catholic Church opposed its women participating in this contest. Their objections proved to have a profound basis: The Catholic hierarchy claimed that it is not the prerogative of society to define what a woman should be, but rather the prerogative of God. They argued that when society assumed the right to define for women what they should be, then that society had usurped the prerogative of God. Personally, I think the Roman Catholics were right. Why should a woman feel inferior because she fails to measure up—or down—to the measurements of Miss America?

In the past, part of the Miss America contest had a question time to ascertain whether a potential candidate for the crown was able to handle the difficult questions people might ask her during her hoped-for reign. In a local contest toward the end of the Vietnam War, the question was asked, "What should be our attitude toward the men who are wearing this country's uniforms while stationed in Vietnam?"

I thought to myself, *That contestant is in trouble now. There is no way she can come out of this alive. If she answers one way, all the hawks will hate her. If she answers the other way, all the doves will hate her. She's doomed to alienate at least half of the audience.*

The contestant then responded, "I really don't know what this war is all about. It all seems so complicated to me. I can't even figure out how we got into this war, but I think that at a time like this we should support our men wherever they are.''

I was intrigued with the answer. What this potential Miss America basically said about herself was that she was stupid and uninformed. The audience loved it because it only affirmed their idea of what an ideal woman is—pretty, but not too intelligent. I thought to myself that she must be pretty smart to act that dumb, and to play the expected role with such precision.

2. *Games women play*. This type of behavior only encourages women to play down their intelligence in order to succeed in a society that is dominated by male chauvinists. Women often tone down their brilliance in order to seem more sexually attractive to men. A study done by one of my graduate students showed that at the time of marriage, the typical man and woman have pretty much the same IQ level. However, after 15 years of marriage, these same women registered about 10 points lower than their husbands. The women had played down their intelligence for so long, and in so many ways, that they had finally become what they pretended to be—not too bright.

I find that the kinds of games women play, to measure up to the culturally prescribed criteria for their successes, are dehumanizing and keep them from growing into the fullness of personhood that God intends for them. When the feminist movement attacks these destructive games, I believe the feminists are condemning behavior that Christ Himself would oppose.

3. *Media images*. The images of females presented in the media are often distorted. Television ads prove to be particularly objectionable for they have a history of depicting women as people who remove dirt. I'm tired of ads where a woman dissolves into tears because her wash isn't as clean as her neighbor's or because she has failed to use a detergent that would remove the ring around her husband's shirt collar. It is no accident that the shows which are aimed at women listeners are called soap operas, since soap is what they usually advertise. The ads depict women as the cleaners in

society, while the ads portray men doing the responsible and important things of life.

Fortunately, the feminist movement has begun to effect some changes in the media. Women are being depicted more and more in roles of leadership and social responsibility. The ads are changing in order to reflect more positive role models for women. This provides encouragement for women considering vocations which in the past were reserved solely for men.

10
Women,
Work,
and the
Feminist Movement

The feminist movement has tried to help women to establish positive identities that are not dependent on the dispositions and attitudes of their husbands. The primary means of achieving these identities are in pursuing vocations outside the home. The feminists have urged women to take positions in the professions so that their sense of worth and success can be from their own accomplishments, rather than from those of their husbands.

In former times, the primary reason for a woman working outside the home was to supplement the family income. Indeed, with inflation being what it is, a wife may have to go to work just to make ends meet. However, the women's movement suggests that vocations will help women to establish positive self-identities. Such a proposal has posed a host of serious problems.

Reentry

Many women face serious emotional strains as they struggle through what has come to be called *the reentry problem*. They have lived for decades in a protected environment that served as a buffer against the competitive struggles of the business world. In many cases their husbands have made most of the important decisions governing the family.

The woman who decides to leave the safety of her domestic cocoon and venture out into a competitive vocational environment may find herself extremely threatened. The feminist movement has tried to assist such women by providing assertiveness-training courses, reentry programs, and seminars. These programs are meant to help women rediscover the ability to be competitive.

Many women were employed in the early years of their marriages, but gave up their jobs when they became mothers. After several years as homemakers, they find it frightening to move back into the world of business and industry.

Several years ago, my wife went through the process of applying for a job at a publishing company. She described how uncomfortable she felt as she went to be interviewed by the director of the personnel department. The sleek professionalism of this young woman made my wife feel inept and inadequate. The youthful arrogance of that personnel director may have been an attempt to cover up her own feelings of inferiority, but nevertheless, she made my wife feel so bad about herself that she came home in tears. Obviously, my wife needed strengthening if she were to go back and try again. (I should hasten to note that my wife's threatened feelings had nothing to do with her capabilities. She subsequently went into real estate sales and enjoyed high earnings in the first year.)

The feminist movement has endeavored to provide support groups made up of women who are going through the reentry experience. These support groups enable women to encourage each other, and thereby facilitate the reentry process.

1. Consciousness-raising and assertiveness training. There is no doubt in my mind but that churches should become involved in helping women to cope with today's problems. Christians are called upon to "bear one another's burdens, and thus fulfill the law of Christ" (Gal. 6:2). It seems to me that every church should form a consciousness-raising group where women can share their fears and aspirations with others who will understand and encourage them.

It is important that such groups exist within a community of believers so that women do not become seduced by anti-Christian value systems. Christian women must learn how to assert themselves without hating those individual chauvinistic males who have in the past put them down and held them back. Women need to learn how to assert themselves without becoming antagonistic toward men as a group. They must be encouraged to assert themselves without assuming the destructive aggressiveness that has too often been a part of the male vocational lifestyle.

2. Positive image for the working mother. Churches can further assist women who face the reentry problem by providing teachings which give them a positive self-image. Too often, I have heard sermons which blame most of the evils of our society on the fact that a significant proportion of American women are gainfully employed outside the home. Uninformed preachers too easily associate drug addiction, juvenile delinquency, teenage pregnancy, and other social problems with the fact that more than one half of American women are now in the work force.

It is true that every child has the right to find a parent at home waiting for him or her at the end of a school day, but this parent need not be the mother. The important thing is that one of the parents should be there to greet the child, wipe the tears if it's been a bad day, provide the traditional glass of milk and cookies, and supervise the late afternoon activities. In many cases, when both husband and wife are working, the couple may find that it is more convenient for the father to be home to greet the children.

Careful study by sociologists has pointed out that in many cases a mother employed outside the home can be a better mother. If a woman finds keeping house to be an unfulfilling vocation, it is better for her to secure a job that offers her emotional satisfaction. Her house may not be as clean as a home maintained by a full-time homemaker, but a perfectly kept house does not guarantee happy and well-adjusted children.

Otto Pollack, former professor of family studies at the University of Pennsylvania, suggests that many women who are homemakers despise keeping house and are filled with resentment because they find themselves trapped into this role by circumstances beyond their control. They may unconsciously suppress that resentment but still it will express itself in many subtle and nonverbal ways. Children, who are better at picking up nonverbal communication signals than adults, read this resentment in their mothers and are deeply affected by it. Pollack suggests that awareness of parental resentment creates emotional disturbances in children, and results in a variety of problems that surface later in life.

According to Pollack, it is better for women to find fulfillment in vocations outside the home rather than to communicate repressed resentments to their children. It is more important that a child come home to a happy mother, than to an immaculately kept house.

Many churches are taking a more enlightened view on women in the work force. They sometimes provide day-care centers and nursery schools in order to help women who have jobs in business and industry. Such private day-care centers have become increasingly necessary as a number of publicly financed centers have closed.

Recent studies indicate that slightly more than half of all the children in the United States are presently being reared in one-parent homes. Usually that parent is the mother. While we wish the situation were otherwise, the fact remains that there are millions of mothers working outside the home who need the assistance of caring churches.

Female Life Expectancy and Identity

A very obvious condition that emerged at the turn of the century should have stimulated us to provide training and encouragement for women who desire vocations other than homemaking. This condition is the increasing life expectancy of women—now at 75. There is, therefore, a prolonged period in their lives after the last child leaves home.

In former centuries, women married relatively early and immediately began their families. The last child left home as the woman approached 50 years of age. Since she usually did not live much longer, raising children became a primary reason for existence.

In today's world, the average woman has two children, who are gone by the time she is 45 years old. What is she to do in her last 30 years? If she thinks of herself only as a mother, these 30 years can be empty and meaningless. This is particularly true if the woman is later divorced, widowed, or separated from her husband.

Churches should be encouraging women to prepare for vocations that will provide meaning and fulfillment in those later years. Instead, many churches contend that "A woman's place is in the home," as though this were a biblically prescribed principle. Actually, there is nothing in the Bible to demand that a woman be limited to the role of homemaker. Biblical women plowed fields, planted vineyards, and worked in the marketplace.

The feminists argue that a woman who does not have a means of establishing identity, other than that provided by her husband, is in an emotionally precarious position. If her husband passes negative judgment on her, and she still keeps trying to carry out her traditionally assigned roles, she will find herself psychologically devastated. The feminists point out that there are few people as pathetic as women married to men who show little or no appreciation for what they are and do.

I know of one woman with five children whose husband became romantically interested in someone else. As this extramarital affair developed, he treated his wife with increasing harshness. He made disparaging remarks about the way she kept house, complained about the quality of food at each meal, criticized the way she raised the children, and made snide remarks about her ability to perform sexually. Her whole self-concept was tied to his view of her; he alone was the significant other in her life, and when he began to define her in a negative way, she developed an increasingly poor self-image. She would go out of her way to do special things for him, and then would wait with bated breath for some positive response. Unfortunately, he had already made up his mind not to like anything she did. He eventually succeeded in turning her into a groveling and humiliated woman who thought of herself as less than nothing.

This woman finally joined a consciousness-raising group with some feminists who helped her to realize what a fine person she really was. As she completed a college education and became a high school social worker, her self-image improved significantly. Once more there was an air of joy about her. Her marriage was still a failure, but it no longer devastated her as it had before. The social adjustment of her children improved vastly, and they became more successful in their schoolwork.

What surprised me was that her pastor condemned her for not staying home and caring for her children; he even inserted snide remarks about people like her in his sermons. Eventually, she left the church. There was no point in taking verbal abuse from someone pretending to proclaim the Word of God.

The church should have provided the kind of help that the feminist group gave this woman. The church that is equipped to provide such services has the capacity to do a much better job. Unfortunately, the feminists encouraged the woman to hate her husband. The church could have taught her how to become a self-realized person without hating anyone.

Mothers of Rebellious Children

Most mothers associate their sense of success and failure with how their children turn out. Unfortunately, there are many children who ruin their own lives or fail to measure up to their potential. In such instances, parents, and especially mothers, have a tendency to accept total blame. Then there is always some religious biddy or cantankerous church leader who self-righteously says: "Train up a child in the way he should go. . . ." (See Proverbs 22:6.)

I would be the last to suggest that parents do not exercise a very significant influence on the development of their children. However, in today's society, parents may not be the decisive influence. Sociologists point out that in the early years of schooling, the values, orientation, and lifestyles of school teachers may be the most important conditioning factors in the lives of many children.

Through the adolescent years, the peer group may prove to be the most important personality-forming factor. Some parents find that, in spite of all they do to bring up their children in the nurture and admonition of the Lord, their children choose friends whose lifestyles are opposed to Christian values. The parents may do their best to bring their children into contact with young people whom the parents feel would have more of a positive influence, only to find that their children are turned off by these more wholesome young people.

When a mother has done and said all that she can, and has provided the best possible example for her children, she must learn to resign herself to the fact that her children are individuals with free wills. They are quite capable of rebelling against everything that she is and advocates. Children are not as easily molded by parents as some people think. Mothers must not condemn themselves too harshly when their children fail. They need to remember that even Mary, the mother of Jesus, had sons who were not believers in the Christ.

I predict that the next decade will witness a parents' rebellion against a society that has harshly held them accountable for their children's behavior. The comment, "There are no delinquent children, just delinquent parents," is scientifically unsound and has created too many unnecessary guilt trips for too many self-effacing mothers.

Warnings about the Feminist Movement

There are several warnings that Christian women should heed as they face the challenges and the promises of the feminist movement.

1. Homemaking is of value. No woman should be conned into feeling that being a homemaker is a worthless and inferior vocation. While some women find that this vocation holds little emotional fulfillment, it must be noted that for many women, keeping house and caring for children is a full-time job and provides all of the emotional gratification they could ever hope to have. While I support those who feel that their personal fulfillment requires an escape from homemaking as a full-time job, I also want to lend encouragement to those women who find it a high and holy calling. While a woman should not feel obligated to be a full-time homemaker simply by virtue of her sexual identity, she should feel free to deliberately choose this role if she believes it to be the vocation to which God has called her.

Too often feminists have overstated their cry for liberation from the traditional role expectations, leaving women who enjoy that traditionally prescribed lifestyle feeling guilty and ashamed because they don't want to be anything other than homemakers. I advocate freedom for women to pursue the leading of the Holy Spirit into that vocation which God has willed for them. It is my prayer that women may enjoy that ecstasy which comes to those who feel that their life's work is important, challenging, and ordained of God.

2. The working world has its problems. Women must be warned not to fall into the same traps that have ensnared men in their vocational involvements. Too often, women in their late 30s have been inspired to reenter the work force, only to find that job opportunities are scarce, and possibilities for advancement limited.

Many women have returned to college in order to gain the

credentials for some prestigious position. They have worked day and night to hold house and home together while pursuing degrees, and the dream that has kept them going was that some day they would have positions of respect and would be able to earn a good living. Unfortunately, many of these women, upon graduation, found that they were entering a job market glutted with white collar professionals. They were left angry by their failure to gain "exciting" jobs.

Many sociologists insist that our population is overly qualified for the kinds of jobs available. There is a surplus of people for positions in education, social services, and communications, while our society finds itself in desperate need of mechanics, draftsmen, and laborers. When women leave the role of homemaking, they are moving into a vocational world which involves considerable risk.

3. A family may not be supportive. A woman may have a long, difficult task in getting the other members of her family to accept her legitimate right to pursue a vocation that makes her feel successful. Even if they lend her verbal encouragement, they are not about to give up the easy life that her full-time attention to homemaking has provided. They will still expect her to wash the clothes, do the dishes, clean the house, and do all the other things that she has always done. They are willing to affirm her new vocational aspirations as long as she still performs all of those tasks that have been traditionally ascribed to women.

Too often a working woman's husband comes home at the end of a day, throws himself into a stuffed chair, and says, "I've had a hard day! When will supper be ready?"

She feels like screaming, *I've had a hard day too. Nobody's making dinner for me. Why don't you come in here and help?*

Husbands and children need to recognize their responsibility to become part of the housekeeping work force when the mother goes out to get a job. They need to see that she cannot go through a role change without all of them simultaneously experiencing changes in their lifestyles. In all probability, it is going to take a lot of patient reeducation to enable typical families to go through this period of transition.

4. *Vocation does not give identity.* Women need to realize that their identities should not ultimately be tied to their vocational employment. If this is allowed to happen, women, like many men, will be threatened with a loss of identity whenever their jobs are phased out or taken from them. Only those people who achieve identity through their relationships with God are able to stand the threats and buffeting which are part of life.

When people recognize God as the ultimate Significant Other, they define their worth in terms of their relationship with Him. When individuals come to love themselves as Jesus does, their sense of self-worth cannot be taken away, no matter what the world does. If they are faithful to their divine calling, a sense of success will pervade their lives, even if the world labels them failures.

11
Single People and Success

In America, one of the symbols of success is a happy family. We try to convince the world that our families are more important than anything we can achieve in our workaday vocations. We like to say that money, fame, and power are of no significance unless our families are happy. We claim that our jobs are only a means to provide for the well-being of our loved ones.

While such rhetoric is lofty, the lifestyles of many people contradict their words. How else can we explain the fact that families are often neglected, as fathers work long hours to gain desired promotions? How else can we explain the countless married couples whose pursuit of success symbols leaves them too exhausted for any kind of intimate relationships? How else can we explain the many young people who, feeling that they don't measure up to their parents' expectations, fall into deep states of depression and seek escape by espousing a countercultural lifestyle?

While few people are willing to admit it openly, their personal successes are usually more important than their families. Nevertheless, an attractive mate and bright, adorable children are necessary display objects for the successful person. William Whyte, Jr., in his book, *The Organization Man*, argues that very often parents want their children to succeed, primarily because of the way that success will reflect upon them. Whyte suggests that the father cheering for his son at the Little League game is not so much concerned about the boy's delight in hitting a home run, as he is about the way in which his son's success will reflect upon him. He looks forward to bragging about it the next time somebody asks, "How are your kids doing?"

For a man, the family often becomes a primary means of displaying what he has achieved. How can he show the world that he has made it unless he provides a good home for his family, fine education for his children, and all the other things that the media suggest every good family should possess?

Singleness Is Disappointing

All of this leaves the single person in a very threatened position. If successful people are happily married, living in split-level houses in suburbia and having beautiful children who go to summer camp, then how can the single person be successful? An individual may achieve power, gain wealth, and hold a position of prestige, but if he has failed to marry, he becomes an object of pity.

We have all noticed how parents speak with disappointment about their unmarried children. Even as they tell about the daughter who has become a surgeon, or the son who is a prominent lawyer, we are aware that they would be happier if their children were married, even though socially less prominent. Parents make children feel guilty for not providing them with grandchildren. Few single career people can evade the fact that in spite of all they have accomplished, they have disappointed their parents in a very essential way.

Single people must constantly cope with friends who are trying to arrange marriages for them. These friends believe that this is the best way to "help" the single individual. The thought seldom occurs to them that singleness may be a chosen way of life.

Single people are made to feel like failures in our society. Parents are disappointed in them, and friends pity them. Society at large is embarrassed by their presence. If there is a dinner party, it is for couples. When we invite a single person, out of necessity or kindness, we usually look for a partner of the opposite sex so that the two can be more socially acceptable as a couple. Even churches are embarrassed by the presence of single adults. The church is so strongly oriented to family life that we don't know what to do with these "spare" people. The church sponsors couples' clubs, family life conferences, and Sunday School classes for those who are married, but very few activities for single people.

Churches here and there have attempted to correct this condition by starting single adult groups. Sometimes these gatherings provide a good social outlet. However, some groups seem to be aimed at matching people up for marriage. Many single people claim that these activities leave them depressed because of an unspoken awareness running through the group that "We're losers."

Single by Choice

What many of us find hard to grasp is that singleness can be a chosen way of life. The Apostle Paul taught that single people are more free to serve God than are those who are married. Paul made the point that the married person finds his loyalties divided between what is pleasing to God and what is necessary to please one's mate. When children come, the problem becomes more complex. Every decision that a parent makes about how to live, and where to work or buy a house, is conditioned by how the children will be affected. Paul wrote,

> I want you to be free from concern. One who is unmarried is concerned about the things of the Lord, how he may please the Lord, but one who is married is concerned about the things of this world, how he may please his wife and his interests are divided. And the woman who is unmarried, and the virgin, is

concerned about the things of the Lord, that she may be holy in both body and spirit; but one who is married is concerned about the things of the world, how she may please her husband (1 Cor. 7:32–34).

I have sensed the conflict that exists in people who want to live sacrificially for God and at the same time want to provide the good life for their families. I too have fallen under conviction as I examine my affluent suburban lifestyle. I think I would move into an inner city situation where I could cast my lot with oppressed peoples, if it were not for the fact that I am married and have children. When I think of moving into a setting that would demand sacrificial living, I have to ask, "Would that situation be safe for my family? What kinds of schools would my children attend?" I know that many missionaries worry about the welfare of their children when trying to decide whether to serve the Lord in some backward Third World nation. Having observed what has happened to a number of missionary children, I am convinced that in many instances it would have been better if these persons had remained childless or had not gone to the field. I have seen too many young people whose psychological adjustments have been difficult, because their parents reared them in remote places.

Single and Ministering

For a number of years I have been associated with a particular Latin American country, where I share in a variety of missionary enterprises. When it comes to ministering to the poor and oppressed people who live in the slums of the city or in the dilapidated villages in the countryside, I find that the Roman Catholic priests are in a better position to minister than are missionaries who go to the field married and with children. The Protestant missionary family usually lives in a house that is considered affluent by the masses of poor people surrounding them. This difference in lifestyle can cause alienation, and prevent effective ministry. On the other hand, the priests, unencumbered by wives and children, are able to live in the midst of the slums and adopt lifestyles that make people aware that these servants of God are one with them in every way. I am not suggesting that this is what all priests do, but only that they are more able to do this than are missionaries who have to care for families.

Roman Catholicism has always glorified the choice of singleness, if that choice is made in order to serve Christ and other people. It is about time for Protestant Christians to recognize that the Bible does teach singleness as the preferred state. Paul admonished Christians to stay single if at all possible: "I wish that all men were as I am. But each man has his own gift from God; one has this gift, another has that. Now to the unmarried and the widows I say: It is good for them to stay unmarried, as I am. But if they cannot control themselves, they should marry, for it is better to marry than to burn with passion" (1 Cor. 7:7–9, NIV).

I have heard theologians and biblical scholars try to give reasons why, in spite of these verses, marriage is the preferred state for the believer. I personally feel that such theologies are rationalizations evading an obvious biblical truth. The ideal lifestyle for Christians was set by One who was single.

In light of this, people often ask me, "Then why are you married?" I am married because I need to be. Life without my wife would be unthinkable. And that is the point the Apostle Paul was trying to make: There are some people who have to be married, but if you are going to serve Jesus in difficult places, it is better to be single. Protestant Christianity should provide special praise for those who choose to remain single in order to serve Christ more effectively. Instead of labeling them as failures, as we subtly do, we should be affirming these single people as the most successful followers of Christ.

Single and Miserable

There are people who are single by no choice of their own. They would like to be married, and they feel very frustrated because they have failed to meet a member of the opposite sex who would be a desirable mate. I know Christians who could have married had they been willing to settle for partners who did not share their Christian convictions. But they decided to adhere to the admonition of Scripture not to be unequally joined to nonbelievers. (See 2 Corinthians 6:14.)

Even so, these people feel left out because other Christians have found partners. They wonder why they have not been as fortunate, and may repress envy as they view their married friends.

Some single adults go through periods of seriously questioning their own worth as persons, asking, "What's wrong with me? Why don't people find me attractive? Why am I such a loser?"

Such questioning can immobilize them, leaving them in a state of depression. They are faced with the ugly reality that our society specializes in superficiality. Hollywood has glorified glamor, and the unglamorous people get left out of the marriage market. A statement such as, "Looks aren't everything," does not alleviate pain for people who are suffering rejection because they lack the face or figure to "turn on" members of the opposite sex.

Is it a source of comfort to recognize that Jesus looks for an inner beauty that is not conditioned by the culturally prescribed criteria for attractiveness? One of my good friends, who is a single female, cried, "I find little comfort in knowing that Jesus thinks I'm beautiful, when none of the men I like think that I am."

I wish there were words I could say that would leave her feeling better. There are men with enough sense to see the beauty of her heart, and I hope and pray that she meets one of them.

Some people perceive their singleness as the failure of God. I have been asked, "Why did God let me down like this? Why didn't He plan for me to have a husband? If marriages are arranged in heaven, why didn't He arrange one for me?"

I do not presume to know the mind of God, nor am I able to grasp how His will is worked out in the world. I do want to point out that God does not manipulate people as though they were robots. He does not make the "right" person marry the "right" person. Whatever God may have planned before the foundation of the world is beyond my knowledge. I do know that what He has planned for us is not always what happens to us.

The Apostle Paul did not speak of mate selection as if it were the result of some celestial mating computer. There is almost a casualness in the way he described how an individual should take a marital partner. Paul seems to be saying that you get married because you like somebody and it seems right to marry that person. I think that we have come to blame too many things on God. Being left in the marriage market should not be one of them.

Single and Worthy

Those who have not chosen singleness, but find themselves unmarried, can pursue a number of courses of action to enhance their feelings of worth. Many single people compensate for not being married by achieving greater success in their vocational sphere. The career teacher may be able to devote more time and attention to students than a married teacher could. The single scholar may be able to achieve successes in research that will more than compensate for not marrying. Indeed, many people have seized upon their singleness and made it an asset instead of a liability.

Singles in Community

A very interesting and hopeful lifestyle for single people has begun to emerge—Christian community. One Presbyterian church in my neighborhood has encouraged groups of single people to buy houses and live together as families. Six women following the advice of the pastor have established such a home. In another house four men have adopted the same plan. These people are finding that their loneliness is dispelled. They have the emotional support of people who are committed to them, and they never lack partners with whom they can share social life. I have watched these people enjoy companionship for vacations and holidays. I think the option they have chosen is not only good but also one that God would desire.

The individuality that forces us to live alone is a dimension of the American culture and not an outgrowth of biblical teaching. I believe the Christian life was meant to be lived in community, and that in establishing community, these single people are more fully approximating God's will. I am not saying that you cannot be a Christian and live alone, but I am saying that as a Christian you should not *want* to live alone. Christianity is a lifestyle of sharing and self-giving. Many Christians are finding that community living is one of the best ways to work out these imperatives.

As I talk to many single people, I find that one of their most common fears is facing the later years of their lives alone. Singles who develop a community in which there is deep binding commitment are delivered from that anxiety.

Another advantage of living in community is that it can provide a wholesome environment for the adoption of children. In most states the law does not necessitate marriage as a precondition for adoption. The six women I mentioned have adopted three children, and are providing a good and happy home for them. The women are overjoyed and the children are blooming.

Most touching is that one of the adopted children is physically handicapped. These six women working together have provided a better home for him than could have been given by a married couple. The extra work involved in rearing this handicapped little boy is shared by the women, and none of them is overburdened by the responsibility. The parents of the six women treat the adopted children as grandchildren. The singleness of these women has not deterred them from finding happiness, or feeling that their lives are successful.

Single and Sexual

As we try to understand what single people face as they live in a world that tends to view singleness as a personal failure, we need to consider the subject of sexuality as it relates to single people.

James H.S. Bossard, my sociology professor at the University of Pennsylvania, called this ''the age of the pure orgasm.'' By that he meant that people have been conned into believing they can never be fulfilled as persons unless they have an active sex life. Indeed, some followers of Masters and Johnson suggest that pleasurable intercourse is a prerequisite for feeling fulfilled as a human being.

I have read several Christian writers who approve of masturbation as a means for single people to gain a sense of sexual fulfillment. These writers have suggested that such behavior is not contrary to the will of God and that single Christians should overcome the guilt which they have for so long associated with the practice.

From a sociological point of view, certain things cause us to question this practice. Social scientists have learned that most people fantasize while they are masturbating. They tend to imagine themselves having intercourse with attractive persons. One woman, while masturbating, usually pretended that she was having intercourse with a former fiance now married to another woman. She wanted to know if what she was doing was a form of adultery. She was disturbed about the teachings of Jesus who said, ''You have heard that it was said, 'Do not commit adultery.' But I tell you that anyone who looks at a woman lustfully has already committed adultery with her in his heart'' (Matt. 5:27, NIV).

Another fact that some social scientists now understand is that the craving for orgasm declines in people who cease having them. The less often an individual has an orgasm, the less often he craves one. The reverse is also true. The more an individual engages in activity that leads to orgasm, the more intensified the desire becomes.

The single person who is not engaging in sexual activity that leads to orgasm in all probability will not live with a high level of frustration.

Divorce

Divorce is a failure. A couple experiencing divorce realizes that what they had hoped for at the time of their marriage has not come true.

An individual involved in a divorce will often feel guilty, and go through intense self-evaluation trying to determine his responsibility for what happened. Anyone looking for a reason to blame himself for a broken marriage undoubtedly will find it. In any marriage, the participants do and say things which hurt the relationship. Should the marriage fail, the guilt associated with that behavior can become inordinate.

1. Self-condemnation. There are some people, usually out of Christian backgrounds, who have an unhealthy tendency toward self-condemnation. They have been brought up not to find fault with others when anything goes wrong, but always to ask, "How did I fail? What did I do wrong?"

A divorce encourages the individual who is overly self-condemning to conclude that he or she is totally responsible for what happened and to label himself or herself a failure. That person's self-esteem drops to such an unparalleled nadir that it becomes difficult to overcome feelings of worthlessness.

If the divorced person has been abandoned or rejected by the former mate, feelings of worthlessness are even more intensified. Such an individual may feel completely unlovable, and unworthy of anyone's attention or concern. One woman I know, whose husband deserted her and their three children in order to pursue a woman who worked in his office, made it clear to me that she thought the divorce was all her fault. "After all," she said, "you wouldn't expect him to stay with somebody as unattractive as I am. I'm such a klutz that it's no wonder he left me."

2. Childrearing. The divorced person left with children to raise only has the problem compounded. Coming out of a marriage that failed, the solitary parent is usually threatened with the fear of also failing in childrearing. Raising children is difficult enough, even when each parent has the support of a sympathetic mate; raising children alone may seem like an almost impossible task.

Very often a divorced mother lacks the financial means to run a successful home because the court has ordered child support payments which are too limited, or because payments ordered rarely appear. It is hard to feel like anything but a failure when she lacks the means to provide an adequate lifestyle for her children. Furthermore, trying to be both mother and father can leave the individual totally exhausted, and consequently, depressed. Depression causes an even greater sense of failure and distorts evaluations of personal worth.

Just for the record, sociological studies conclusively show that children who are raised by a divorced parent have just as good a chance of achieving a healthy emotional and psychological adjustment as a child reared in an intact family. This is good news especially since recent government statistics indicate that slightly more than half of America's children are raised in single-parent homes, the majority of which are created by divorce. These statistics should convince the divorced parent that his children are not unusual because they are being raised by one parent.

3. The church. The victims of unsuccessful marriages are broken people who need to be put back together again by the church. However, the church, instead of providing part of the solution for these people, often becomes part of the problem. Sometimes church members enhance the guilt feelings felt by the divorced people in their congregations. They may do this by acting as though the divorced persons should have stayed with their mates regardless of the consequences, and in spite of the fact that their mates may not have wanted them. These members make such statements as, "She should have stayed with him for the sake of the children, if for no other reason."

Studies indicate, to the contrary, that being raised by a single divorced parent gives a child a much greater chance of achieving emotional and psychological well-being than if that child is raised in what some social scientists call "an empty shell marriage."

The Bible does not prohibit divorce. The Scriptures recognize that a marriage can become intolerable. "To the married, I give this command (not I, but the Lord): A wife must not separate from her husband. But if she does, she must remain unmarried or else be reconciled to her husband. And a husband must not divorce his wife" (1 Cor. 7:10–11, NIV).

Some scholars suggest that even the Apostle Paul may have suffered a divorce. We know he was married because he was a member of the Jewish Sanhedrin, and marriage was a prerequisite for membership in that august body. These scholars pose that after his conversion, Paul and his wife may have separated because she could not adhere to his new lifestyle and belief. While this is speculation, some people wonder if an unhappy marriage could be part of the reason Paul extolled singleness as a preferred state.

4. *Remarriage.* The probability that a divorced person will remarry is relatively high. Divorced people are more likely to get married than are single people of the same age. Increasingly, the church is having to deal with divorced and remarried persons in its membership, recognizing that such persons are no longer isolated curiosities, but a common presence.

The problem that most Christians have with the divorce issue stems from the explicit teachings of Jesus on the subject. " 'Therefore what God has joined together, let man not separate.' When the disciples asked Jesus about this, He answered, 'Anyone who divorces his wife, except for marital unfaithfulness, and marries another woman commits adultery' " (Matt. 19:6, 8, NIV).

It is hard to get around these verses if one holds to the Bible as being inspired by the Holy Spirit. And it is easy to see why so many Christians categorically condemn divorced people who have remarried.

On the more liberal side of the issue, there are many who contend that Christians should be gracious toward the divorced and the remarried. They argue that Jesus is the Lord of the second chance, a Saviour who offers to people both forgiveness for their mistakes and an opportunity to start over again.

There are those who argue that social practices like divorce and remarriage must be understood in light of the times in which they were established. In the ancient world a divorced woman was usually abandoned with no means of support. Often she had to resort to prostitution to survive. Divorce left her without dignity and rights, so that no Christian would ever reduce his marital partner to such a dehumanized condition. Since the times and conditions have changed, the argument goes, so should our pronouncements on divorce.

Others say that divorce is only a legal arrangement that permits the individual to take another mate but does not absolve the partner from responsibility for the well-being of his or her former spouse, until death parts them. In short, while the individual may be separated or divorced from the original mate, there is still a responsibility to see to it that the person has his or her economic needs met and is the recipient of concern until the end of life. The claim is made that the individual who fulfills these responsibilities has upheld the basic intent of Jesus' teachings.

I do not believe the problem can be resolved so simply. But I have learned to accept my divorced and remarried friends as brothers and sisters in Christ. While I do not encourage remarriage, I try not to be judgmental toward these people.

5. *Principled and gracious.* I think the church is obligated to accept the difficult challenge of upholding a principle, on the one hand, and being gracious to the violators, on the other. This is extremely difficult, because graciousness to violators can easily be interpreted as laxity concerning the principle. The church must stand opposed to divorce and remarriage, yet remain accepting and open toward those who violate the principle.

Jesus demonstrated this balance when the Pharisees brought to Him a woman "caught in the very act" of adultery. The teachings of Scripture called for the stoning to death of a woman caught in adultery. Rather than being judgmental, Jesus showed grace to the woman, forgave her, and gave her a new start in life. (See John 8:1–11.)

No one could ever accuse Jesus of being lax concerning biblical principles. He stood on trial before Pilate, as One who had not violated the Law in any way, and in whom no one could find any fault. But this same Jesus who came to fulfill the Law, not to destroy it, constantly showed grace to those who had failed to uphold the Law and needed a new beginning. When He met Zaccheus, He did not condemn, but rather showed loving acceptance of a man whose lifestyle would have been judged severely by the religious legalists of his day.

Widowhood

The death of a mate can deal a serious blow to the survivor's will to live. What does it matter if you have money, power, and social respect if the most important human being in your life is snatched from you? Many people are able to define themselves as successful because their mates, as significant others in their lives, have made them feel successful in spite of the discouragement and buffeting encountered in the world. In more cases than we can imagine, the death of a marital partner leaves an individual without the one person who has made him or her feel significant and successful.

The loss of a mate is particularly hard on a woman whose position in society was gained through marriage. For such a woman, the husband's death is not only the loss of a partner, but also a major threat to her own social status.

I know of one pastor's wife who experienced a complete breakdown after her husband died. Her whole identity had been wrapped up in her claim that she was married to the most prominent religious leader in the community. Being the minister's wife had made her a prime candidate for every women's club, and a leader of several organizations in the church. The community had viewed her and her husband as a team in ministry, and rightly so. She had played the organ, led the choir, was an officer in the women's group, and had run the junior youth fellowship. Suddenly, her husband died of a heart attack. Not only did this woman lose her husband but also her social identity as well.

She tried to remain a member of the same church, but this proved to be a problem to everyone. The wife of the new pastor quickly replaced her in many of those positions which had been such a part of her life. The new pastor, feeling nervous about having his predecessor's wife as the director of music, maneuvered her out of that position as quickly as possible. The widow went into a depression that required psychiatric treatment. Her depression was the result of loss, not only of her dear husband but also of the success symbols that were associated with her role as his wife.

Persons facing this kind of a loss find it almost impossible to overcome the pain of the situation without the help of others. A church fellowship must recognize responsibility to provide a new and positive self-image to the widow, and in many cases, to the widower. Persons who have suffered the loss of mates need to feel an identity and significance all their own and know that their worth stands apart from the status of their former partners. It is the task of the church to discover their personal gifts and encourage them to use these gifts in service for others. Furthermore, the church should pour out appreciation to these people for what they do and who they are.

When I was a young pastor, one of my greatest failings was in not pronouncing publicly my gratitude for the many things that elderly widows and widowers did to serve the church. Every congregation in America should be bending over backwards to make these people feel appreciated.

Churches that are trying to be true to their calling should heed the words of the Apostle James: "This is pure and undefiled religion in the sight of our God and Father, to visit orphans and widows in their distress, and to keep oneself unstained by the world" (James 1:27). One of the most positive helps to widows and widowers that I have seen has been established by a former minister and denominational executive who has given himself full time to helping people who are alone. He has brought several hundred such people together in an organization to help them cope with their new condition.

This group not only helps widows and widowers, but also the divorced, who likewise experience a loss of social identity when they step out of the bonds of marriage. Unlike some efforts to minister to such people, this group does not exist for the purpose of matchmaking or providing socials for lonely people. Instead, its purpose is to counsel each person through the difficult transition to the establishment of an identity apart from the former mate. In this group individuals can openly and honestly share the pains and struggles of their attempts to adjust.

Too often, the only way the church knows to alleviate the loneliness of those who have lost mates is to marry them off to some new partners. The tendency to play matchmaker is more intense when the widows or widowers are relatively young. But often such good intentions can result in hurting people even more. The efforts are interpreted as evidence that they cannot arrange their own lives or are incapable of attracting members of the opposite sex on their own.

Widowed persons frequently have no desire to enter into new marriages. While their marriages were happy, some widows and widowers don't feel that they have the time and energy to go through the whole adjustment process again. It would be better if the church concentrated on helping these people to gain positive identities and to sense worthwhile accomplishments that are explicitly their own.

The death of a partner leaves the widow or widower feeling that there was so much more that could have been done for the deceased. People in this situation often feel that they failed to be the marital partner they could have been. They remember all the things that they said and did which cannot be erased. They are even more aware of what they failed to say or do. With such feelings of failure, these individuals need assurance that God forgives and forgets.

One of the most comforting doctrines of Scripture is the good news that God has blotted out our sins and remembers them no more. Those who are with Him take on His character; loved ones now with the Lord can forget the wrongs that happened in this world. I believe that in the afterlife, the negative things that transpired between marital partners will not be remembered.

12
The
Throwaway People

Growing old in America does not bring the honor and respect that it did in ancient cultures. Ours is a youth-oriented society, and when youth is lost, so is the glamour of living. Consequently, it is no wonder that the cosmetic industry earns billions of dollars each year producing the means by which the aging process can be concealed.

What is true in America is true for all industrial societies. Young people are preferred because they are more adaptable to the rapid changes of the modern world. In preindustrial societies, the elderly were respected because they had mastered craft skills which were the basics of economic production. The young looked with awe toward the elderly who knew how to do with perfection those things which the young wanted to learn.

Retirement

In today's society, old age usually means retirement. For some this may be a welcome period of life, but for most people, it is covertly dreaded. This is particularly true for men whose identities are so wrapped up with their jobs that when they retire, they often lose the clear definition of who they are. People who had positions of social prestige, and enjoyed the deference granted by employees under them, find these symbols of success suddenly gone.

Many retirees don't know what to do with the vast amount of time suddenly on their hands. Always before, life had been intensely organized, every minute of the day full of important tasks that gave a sense of significance. For many men, the fact that they had no time for "trivialities" convinced them that they were people of importance. With retirement, all of that changes, and for many men this free time becomes an unbearable burden.

In my own counseling experience, many elderly women have come to me complaining about their retired husbands who follow them around all during the day. The husbands just don't know what to do with themselves. These women tell me how their once prestigious mates have been reduced to pathetic personalities, simply because they are lost in this new world of leisure time. There is a soaring divorce rate among retired people, and one of the causes cited is that wives cannot cope with husbands who expect to be constantly entertained. What some of these wives do not admit is that they have lost respect for their husbands, now that they no longer have prestigious positions.

Women seem to be able to handle the retirement years more easily. This is particularly true for the middle- and upper-middle-class women who find that the retirement of their husbands does not significantly alter their lifestyles. After the children are raised, many of these women spend as many as 25 years keeping their homes tidy, belonging to garden clubs, attending church activities, and watching television. The retirement of their husbands does not change most of that. Consequently, there is no traumatic transition as they move into the twilight years.

Economic Identity of the Elderly

One of the most depressing aspects of old age in America is that economic factors often cause the elderly to see themselves as worthless and insignificant. Feelings of failure are common among old people confined to small, dilapidated apartments. Inflation lessens the value of their fixed income and diminishes the significance of their savings. People who were once proud of their independence often find themselves dependent on the state for survival. Their grown children, with their own families to care for, often have little left to maintain elderly parents in the manner to which they had been accustomed. Poor elderly people often see themselves as burdens to family and society and simply wait for death. In a society that puts a high premium on success, these people see themselves as failures. They live out their lives feeling that they have come to nothing.

It is no wonder that my wife urges me to figure out ways for us to be wealthy in our old age. She has observed that the elderly who are rich are still respected, taken places, and treated with care and thoughtfulness by their children and relatives. There may be more truth to her observations than I am willing to admit. In many cases, care by others in the waning years of life is dependent upon how much money the elderly person has to will to those others at death.

Retirement Homes

Retirement homes sometimes have disastrous effects on the identity of the elderly. This is not an indictment of all retirement homes; for some, particularly those which are church related, effectively enhance the personal worth of their residents, and enable them to maintain a sense of significance throughout life. However, it is obvious that many establishments for the elderly strip them of dignity and leave them as vegetating creatures who wonder why death doesn't come sooner.

I recall, as a young pastor, visiting an elderly member of my congregation who was residing in a county home for the aged. When I signed in at the reception desk, I noticed from the card that the last time this woman had been visited by anyone was 18 months ago. In the ward, I made my way down an aisle that neatly separated 20 beds. The room was immaculately clean, and the bed linens had been changed that morning. Ample food was provided to the patients and yet there was a sterileness about the ward that immediately depressed me. While the people were being cared for physically, they seemed to be stripped of personhood. In bed after bed were elderly women with glazed looks on their faces. They had handled the absurdity of their plight by emotionally detaching themselves from their environment and traveling via imagination to a time and place when things were better.

I finally found the woman I was seeking, introduced myself, and tried to make pleasant conversation. As the lunch hour approached, a nurse came in to feed the patients. She went to the first bed, pried open the mouth of the elderly occupant, shoved a spoonful in her mouth and yelled, "Swallow it!"

She repeated the process about five times before I mustered the courage to get up from where I was sitting, go over to her, and boldly ask, "Do you have to do it that way?"

She stood up straight, looked down at me and said, "You're a minister, aren't you?"

As a young pastor I prided myself on looking like a "normal" person. Since people were usually shocked to discover that I was a clergyman, I was disappointed at being so easily recognized, and asked, "How did you know?"

She said, "Your kind is always coming in here complaining about the things I do. Mister, I have 40 patients to feed in an hour. I wish I could be gentle, but the limitation on my time forces me to do things in a very unpleasant manner. If you're concerned about the way these women eat, why don't you get the women's group of your church to spend one day a week giving them lunch? It will probably beat what they usually do with their time."

The surprising thing was that when I made that recommendation to the group, the women rejected it. It seemed as though they were more willing to prepare bandage rolls for the suffering people in Africa than to feed the elderly who lived down the street. Why is it that we always find it so much easier to express concern from a distance?

Our society cannot content itself by providing "adequate" care for the elderly in such conditions. The psychological damage experienced in such settings must be a subject for our concern.

Responses to Aging

We should all be aware of two facts. First, as the younger people who are voting and making the decisions that determine the fate of the elderly, we are creating the conditions in which we ourselves must eventually live. And second, Jesus was particularly concerned about the plight of the elderly and often measured commitment to God by the way people treated the elderly widows. I too believe that the measure of our Christian love can be seen in the way in which we treat the elderly.

. The responses of people to the threats of old age have been varied. Many, upon retirement, have moved to areas of the country where there is a warmer climate. For instance, St. Petersburg, Florida has become famous as a residence area for senior citizens. The same can be said about many sections of Southern California. After retirement, an elderly couple can sometimes find excitement and challenge by moving to a new location and "starting life over again." The new setting means new friends, a new church, a new house, and a new lifestyle. These challenges can occupy time and give the elderly significant things to do. What is more, they have excuses for making long trips back home to visit former friends and relatives and report on their happy circumstances in retirement. But this option is available only to those who have a good income.

Some of the elderly have opted for staying put on their old familiar turf. They often find an exciting lifestyle in the activities of a local senior citizens club. Communities all across America have these clubs that sponsor bus trips, picnics, bowling parties, socials, and classes for the elderly.

It is sad when retired people deprive themselves of the enjoyment of such activities simply because they are afraid of the social labels that they think are on people who belong to such organizations. Wanting to perpetuate the myth that they are not old, they refuse to join clubs for the elderly.

The Church and the Elderly

Every church should be either a supporter or sponsor of group activities for senior citizens. The 50 percent of the churches in the United States that have less than 100 members lack the resources to create such programs on their own. But even small churches can enter into cooperative relationships with other churches or community organizations in order to make sure that retirees enjoy the rich, recreational life to which they are entitled.

Churches have a responsibility to honor the elderly who have served them. There should be special recognition dinners, participation in the worship services, and other special ways to let the elderly know the importance of their contributions.

The congregation should not wait until its elderly members die before fellowship halls, Sunday School rooms, or organs are dedicated in their honor. The church can be the significant other for the elderly, reflecting to them such a sense of status that they will feel they have lived successfully, even as life winds down.

Some churches have put retired people to work in significant ways. The elderly make excellent associate pastors, and many congregations have found their ministry enriched by having retired members take on the job of minister of visitation-evangelism. Still other churches have called upon retired members to serve as business managers, thus enhancing the efficiency of the churches' programs. Some retired people have become lay preachers for small congregations that could never afford to pay their pastors. In most cases, these retired people work without salary to make possible ministries which could never be funded by existing church budgets.

The mother of President Jimmy Carter set a blazing example for the elderly by becoming a Peace Corps member in her later years. The U.S. government has come to recognize that elderly people have a vast array of professional skills which are desperately needed in developing nations. Churches would do well to encourage some of their retired members to apply to VISTA or other government agencies for placement overseas. Such positions offer excellent opportunities for the missionary enterprise. Retired people serving in Third World countries can ally themselves with indigenous churches and contribute to the ministry of Christ, while serving as part of a government agency. Such activities can give retired people a greater sense of significance and success than they ever achieved in their preretirement years.

Several church denominations, particularly the Mennonites, have developed a system for placing retired business executives, engineers, and political personnel on the mission field to serve in advisory capacities. Pastors should counsel elderly people to explore such options for the later stages of life.

Gray Panthers

One of the most exciting organizations in America is called the Gray Panthers. This social action group works for positive changes on behalf of the elderly and other groups in our society. The Gray Panthers organize elderly people into consumer-protection pressure groups that go to federal and state legislatures to lobby for lower utility rates and better social services. These senior citizens serve as watchdogs on government, serving the society at large in ways that employed people can never do because of lack of time. The Gray Panthers put pressure on the oil companies on behalf of the rest of us. They make demands on local government, facilitating community improvement. In countless ways, the Gray Panthers help the elderly to achieve a sense of success and worth.

One of the demands of the Gray Panthers is that homes for the elderly be run by the residents rather than by outside boards of directors. This request is particularly aimed at church-related homes. Why should a group of people who do not live in a retirement center make decisions that determine the destiny of the residents?

Since the residents usually finance the retirement homes by willing over to them their remaining resources, why shouldn't they make decisions controlling what happens? Why shouldn't they vote on who should be hired as doctors and nurses? Or determine the structure of the budgets? Or be the ones who hire and fire the working staff?

If the people who serve the elderly in these retirement homes were responsible to the residents rather than to an absentee board, the level of service would be improved and treatment would become increasingly humane. There are elderly residents who have the skills to administer these homes; the awareness of controlling their own destinies would provide them with a deep sense of self-esteem and success.

Some have argued that we ought to do away with retirement communities altogether. They maintain that the elderly prefer to be around the young, to be closer to people who are still active in society. However, many studies argue to the contrary, and show that the elderly fare better when living in communities with other people of the same age, *providing these communities offer a variety of activities and programs for their residents*. I have visited many retirement communities that bristle with excitement, where the residents find themselves more actively involved in the work of Christ and in community service than ever before in their lives.

A Final Word about Value

Ultimately, the church speaks the final word about the value of life. When we face death, much of what we have deemed significant in life appears meaningless. Death forces us to view the worthlessness of so many things that we have worked hard to achieve. We often try to escape its reality by hyperactivity, in the hope that this will protect us against "morbid" reflection. Nevertheless, in the waning years of life, we sense ourselves moving inexorably toward that final threat to the wealth, power, and prestige that we have worked so hard to achieve. One German philosopher writes, "We make so much noise on New Year's Eve because we are trying to drown out the macabre sound of grass growing over our own graves."

The Gospel has good news: What we have attempted to do for Christ and His kingdom will not be lost. We are informed by the Apostle Paul that the good work which Christ has begun in us will continue until the day of His coming. (See Philippians 1:6.) We need to know that our efforts for Christ and His kingdom will not evaporate. The message of God seems to be that it is better to fail in a cause that will ultimately win than to win in a cause that will ultimately fail.

Christians *can* approach death knowing that they have been part of a movement which will triumph in history. Whatever their involvement in the work of God, they will receive their reward. Even those who look upon their labors as insignificant are informed that they shall stand before the ultimate Judge and be told, "Well done, good and faithful servant! You have been faithful with a few things; I will put you in charge of many things" (Matt. 25:21, NIV).

What does death mean for people who do not feel they have served Jesus in any significant way? I can only suggest that Jesus Himself says that many will be surprised on the Day of Judgment as to how much they did accomplish; they fed the hungry, clothed the naked, visited the sick, and ministered to those who were in prison. Jesus will tell them that what they did for the least of the brethren, they did for the Lord Himself. (See Matthew 25:34–40.)

What does death mean for those who are sure they have failed to serve Christ at all? I believe that there will be service that we can render to the Lord after we go to be with Him and throughout eternity, because service is the ultimate form of worship.

To those who approach death with a feeling of failure, I say that there is an endless eternity in which you can succeed for Jesus. All that He asks is that you recognize your salvation as a gift which results from His grace, and is not dependent upon your own achievements. What greater sense of success can you hope for than the awareness that you have, in eternity, an everlasting opportunity to fulfill God's plans for you?

13
A Theology of Success

$\mathbf{A}$ good friend once asked me, "Isn't it true that the person who lives in accord with the will of God, and patterns his life after the teachings of Scripture, can expect to live a successful life?"

My answer was, "Yes, but I am not sure that the kind of success which will be delivered is exactly what you have in mind."

Too many people believe that faith in God and adherence to His laws will deliver wealth, power, and status. They have heard sermons, on radio and television, which suggest that faith in God and obedience to His Word guarantee social success. They imagine that they will move up the socioeconomic ladder by virtue of their goodness. They assume that when the Apostle Paul promises that God will "do exceeding abundantly beyond all that we ask or think, according to the power that works in us" (Eph. 3:20), he means believers will prosper in miraculous ways and lack for nothing in the way of this world's goods.

Will Herberg, a contemporary Jewish social philosopher, claims that Americans have "faith in faith." They think believing in God assures them of economic prosperity and personal achievement. He may be right. But this kind of "faith" makes God a means to our own personal ends and declares that He is there to help us to achieve things which society tells us are important.

The eternal God does not exist to serve our ends. He is not an instrument for the fulfillment of our wishes. We exist to serve Him. We are called to be instruments of His will.

Prayer as Magic

Many sociologists differentiate religion from magic by pointing out that in religion people submit themselves to the will of a higher power; in magic, people try to manipulate a higher power to get things for themselves. Many people who think they have true religion transform the Christian faith into a primitive form of magic, treating God as though He were the genie of the magic lamp. Prayer becomes a litany for manipulating God into delivering what the petitioners want. Jesus' name becomes a magical incantation that must be blasphemously uttered at the end of the prayer if God is to deliver the desired results. For many, prayer reflects the kind of immaturity that my little boy expressed one evening when he came into our living room and said, "Before I go to bed, I'm going to pray. Does anybody want anything?"

A Certain Success

I believe that the Christian lifestyle does deliver success to people, but not the kind of success that is understood by society. Jesus never promised wealth, power, and prestige to those who would follow Him. He warned that while foxes had holes and birds had nests, the disciples were following One who would not have a place to lay His head (Matt. 8:20). He was scorned and rejected by the people of this world. Then as now, the social establishment would crucify Him. Jesus warned His followers that what happened to Him would happen to them.

"If the world hates you, keep in mind that it hated Me first. If you belonged to the world, it would love you as its own. As it is, you do not belong to the world, but I have chosen you out of the world. That is why the world hates you. Remember the words I spoke to you: 'No servant is greater than his master.' If they persecuted Me, they will persecute you also. If they obeyed My teaching, they will obey yours also. They will treat you this way because of My name, for they do not know the One who sent Me'' (John 15:18–21, NIV).

There is truth to the saying, ''When Jesus calls a man, He bids him come and die.''

Perhaps a trip through some of the poor Third World countries would shock Christians who have a Pollyanna theology. They would see a contemporary witness to the fact that godly people do not necessarily get rich. In the back hills of Haiti, I have observed Christians rising at 5:00 in the morning to pray and sing praises to God before they begin their work. The devotion of these people to Christ and their faithful obedience to His Word is an inspiration. Yet, despite their love for Christ and willingness to do His will, these people suffer from terrible poverty and privation. Haitian Christians experience real joy, but it is not based on economics. Life for them *is* successful, but they can't measure that success in status symbols.

Life after Death

The belief that godly people will become economically prosperous and socially honored emerges from a misinterpretation of ancient Orthodox Judaism. The Old Testament Jews had no clear concept of life after death. Many have suggested that Judaism was and is the most existential of all religions, with the rewards of a godly life being experienced in this world in the lifetime of the true believer.

At the time of Christ, the Sadducees—the most orthodox of Jews—held no belief in the afterlife, and mocked Jesus because He did. In an intriguing confrontation, they tried to trap Him by making belief in the life after death seem ridiculous. After telling a story of seven brothers who had all been married to the same woman, the Sadducees asked, '' 'At the resurrection, whose wife

will she be of the seven, since all of them were married to her?'
Jesus replied, 'You are in error because you do not know the
Scriptures or the power of God. At the resurrection people will
neither marry nor be given in marriage; they will be like the angels
in heaven. But about the resurrection of the dead—have you not
read what God said to you, "I am the God of Abraham, the God of
Isaac, and the God of Jacob"? He is not the God of the dead but of
the living' " (Matt. 22:28–32, NIV).

Jesus clearly teaches a life after death, and it is that doctrine
which forces us into a new and deeper understanding of success
and failure. Because this life is brief when compared with eternity,
success and failure cannot be understood within the context of
space and time. Within human history, those who succeed may not
be those who ultimately know success. This is clear in that famous
parable which Jesus gives us concerning the rich man and Lazarus.

There was a rich man who was dressed in purple and fine linen
and lived in luxury every day. At his gate was laid a beggar
named Lazarus, covered with sores and longing to eat what
fell from the rich man's table. Even the dogs came and licked
his sores. The time came when the beggar died and the angels
carried him to Abraham's side. The rich man also died and
was buried. In hell, where he was in torment, he looked up
and saw Abraham far away, with Lazarus by his side. So he
called to him, "Father Abraham, have pity on me and send ˅
Lazarus to dip the tip of his finger in water and cool my
tongue, because I am in agony in this fire." But Abraham
replied, "Son, remember that in your lifetime you received
good things, while Lazarus received bad things, but now he is
comforted here and you are in agony" (Luke 16:19–25, NIV).

The New Testament makes it clear that it may be hard to
perceive the rewards of a godly life this side of heaven, but beyond
the grave the "first will be last; and the last, first" (Matt. 19:30).
Those who are first in status here may not be so honored on the
other side of the grave. The Orthodox Judaism of the Sadducees—

which I believe to be a misinterpretation of the Old Testament—taught that the godly would be prestigious, powerful, and wealthy in this world. However, those who believe in the resurrection and the life everlasting do not find themselves boxed in with such limitations. We Christians believe that for those who are in Christ there is a blessedness which transcends capitalistic value systems, and more than compensates for whatever privations and offenses we may suffer in this life. We, with the Apostle Paul, can say: "I consider that our present sufferings are not worth comparing with the glory that will be revealed in us" (Rom. 8:18, NIV).

Evidence of Election

The misconception that faith in God and obedience to His law automatically deliver wealth, power, and prestige has been derived not only from the Judaism of the Sadducees, but also from some versions of Protestantism. Max Weber, in his classic sociological work, *The Protestant Ethic and the Spirit of Capitalism*, contends that certain Protestants, particularly those in the Calvinistic tradition, have twisted Reformed theology in order to make wealth the evidence of divine election. Through careful historical analysis, Weber points out that there were some Calvinists who wanted concrete evidence that God had chosen them to be saved. The doctrine of predestination declared that God had already decided who would be saved and who would be lost. However, these Calvinists still wondered what the evidences or signs of divine election might be. How would the saved know if they were saved?

Many Christians answered that the saved would know of their election because they would economically prosper. Thus, prosperity became the evidence of a right relationship with God. Weber is not saying that Calvin actually propagated this idea; but it was commonly circulated within the Calvinist tradition. And in this group were the Puritans, who gave birth to this country, providing the character of our culture.

Weber argues that as a result of the Protestant work ethic, people have endeavored to accumulate wealth as a symbol of salvation. The materialism of America has resulted from a belief system that makes economic success evidence of one's personal worth and standing with God. Often without knowing why, people in this tradition work incessantly to accumulate as much money as possible. Subconsciously, they want to assure themselves that they are God's elite. Even though they have more than enough money to live comfortably, they work night and day. For them wealth has a symbolic value that they may not fully understand: It not only provides them with comfort, but also with psychological security. Economic success assures them that they are God's people.

Arrogant Unconcern

Such a belief system can create an arrogance in the wealthy, causing them to look upon the less fortunate with contempt. We have all heard religious people brag, "I started with nothing, but because I worked hard and was thrifty, I got what I have today." This implies that people are poor because they are lazy and wasteful; when the truth may be that poverty is the result of discrimination and economic exploitation. The poor often find themselves the victims of social injustice and psychological oppression by a society that equates their poverty with God's disfavor.

Protestantism vs. Jesus

The value system of many Protestants is described by Max Weber as being diametrically opposed to the attitudes of Jesus. He was a friend of the poor and the needy who heard Him gladly because He gave them good news from the heavenly Father.

Looking at His disciples, He said: "Blessed are you who are poor, for yours is the kingdom of God. Blessed are you who hunger now, for you will be satisfied. Blessed are you who weep now, for you will laugh. Blessed are you when men hate you, when they exclude you and insult you and reject your name as evil, because of the Son of Man. Rejoice in that day and leap for joy, because great is your reward in heaven. For that is how their fathers treated the prophets. But woe to you who are rich, for you have already received your comfort. Woe to you who are well fed now, for you will go hungry. Woe to you who laugh now, for you will mourn and weep" (Luke 6:20–25, NIV).

Jesus was the Incarnation of the eternal God who heard the cries of the oppressed children of Israel and championed their cause against the rich and mighty Pharaoh. Jesus was the same God who caused Amos to warn the rich people of Israel to beware of the Day of Judgment that would come upon them because of their indifference to the plight of the poor.

Jesus made it clear that wealth, instead of being proof of godliness, could easily be a barrier to a rich person hoping to enter the kingdom of heaven.

Jesus looked around and said to His disciples, "How hard it is for the rich to enter the kingdom of God!" The disciples were amazed at His words. But Jesus said again, "Children, how hard it is to enter the kingdom of God! It is easier for a camel to go through the eye of a needle than for a rich man to enter the kingdom of God." The disciples were even more amazed, and said to each other, "Who then can be saved?" Jesus looked at them and said, "With man this is impossible, but not with God; all things are possible with God" (Mark 10:23–27, NIV).

The wealthy person is in a very precarious position when it comes to entering the kingdom. It is hard to see how a person can live in luxury when so many of his brothers and sisters in the world live in degrading poverty.

John Wesley urged Christians to work as hard as they could, to make as much money as they could, in order to give away as much as they could. Wealth, even comparative wealth, is an awesome responsibility. Christians cannot escape the words of Christ: "From everyone who has been given much, much will be demanded; and from the one who has been entrusted with much, much more will be asked'' (Luke 12:48, NIV).

Pulling Down the Blinds

During a visit to Haiti, I went to a restaurant. The waiter seated me by a large window. He took my order and then brought me a very attractive dinner. I was about to eat a bite of steak when I happened to look to my left. Eight hungry Haitian children, with their noses pressed up against the glass, were staring at my food. I immediately lost my appetite and set the fork down. The waiter, seeing what was happening, quickly moved in and pulled down the venetian blind. He said to me, "Enjoy your meal. Don't let them bother you."

I thought to myself, *Isn't that what we all do? We pull down the blinds so we don't have to look at the poor and hungry of the world.*

I believe that God will punish our indifference to the poor. Our wealth, instead of being evidence of our blessedness, will be the cause of our judgment.

Reward in This World

I don't want to suggest that the only positive payoff for a Christian is life beyond the grave. While I do believe in heaven and in hell, let me say that even if these two realities did not exist, I would still be a Christian because of the reward that a commitment to Christ delivers here and now.

I cannot promise wealth, power, and prestige to followers of Christ, but I can say that those who sacrifice financially in His name are rewarded in this world. Those who forego the prestige that the world offers will be blessed in a manner that this world cannot understand. Christians who empty themselves of the need for power and become servants of others in the name of our Lord will experience a joy that knows no bounds.